AF606783

Soup Today

Publications International, Ltd.

Louis Weber, CEO
Publications International, Ltd.
8140 Lehigh Ave
Morton Grove, IL 60053

Pictured on the front cover: Classic Lentil Soup *(page 42).*

Pictured on the back cover *(clockwise from top left):* Chicken Enchilada Soup *(page 94)*, One-Pot Chinese Chicken Soup *(page 87)*, Pasta e Ceci *(page 6)*, Spicy Thai Shrimp Soup *(page 150)* and Beef Barley Soup *(page 126).*

ISBN: 978-1-63938-739-7

Manufactured in China.

8 7 6 5 4 3 2 1

Microwave Cooking: Microwave ovens vary in wattage. Use the cooking times as guidelines and check for doneness before adding more time.

WARNING: Food preparation, baking and cooking involve inherent dangers: misuse of electric products, sharp electric tools, boiling water, hot stoves, allergic reactions, foodborne illnesses and the like, pose numerous potential risks. Publications International, Ltd. (PIL) assumes no responsibility or liability for any damages you may experience as a result of following recipes, instructions, tips or advice in this publication.

While we hope this publication helps you find new ways to eat delicious foods, you may not always achieve the results desired due to variations in ingredients, cooking temperatures, typos, errors, omissions or individual cooking abilities.

Let's get social!

 @Publications_International

 @PublicationsInternational

www.pilbooks.com

Contents

Pasta & Grains

Swiss Orzo Chowder

Makes 4 servings

- 1¼ cups chicken broth
- 1 cup frozen cut green beans
- ½ cup shredded carrot
- ⅓ cup (2 ounces) uncooked orzo pasta
- 1 teaspoon dried basil
- ½ teaspoon salt
- ¼ teaspoon black pepper
- ½ cup sliced yellow squash or zucchini
- 2½ cups milk, divided
- 3 tablespoons all-purpose flour
- ¼ cup (1 ounce) shredded Swiss cheese

1. Combine broth, green beans, carrot, orzo, basil, salt and pepper in medium saucepan; bring to a boil over high heat. Reduce heat to medium-low; cover and simmer 10 minutes.
2. Stir in squash; cover and cook 2 minutes or until vegetables are tender.
3. Whisk ½ cup milk into flour in small bowl until smooth and well blended. Stir into vegetable mixture. Add remaining 2 cups milk; bring to a boil over medium heat, stirring constantly. Boil 1 minute. Stir in cheese; cook and stir just until melted.

Pasta e Ceci

Makes 4 servings

- **4 tablespoons olive oil, divided**
- **1 onion, chopped**
- **1 carrot, chopped**
- **1 clove garlic, minced**
- **1 sprig fresh rosemary**
- **1 teaspoon salt, plus additional for seasoning**
- **1 can (28 ounces) whole tomatoes, drained and crushed (see Tip)**
- **2 cups vegetable broth**
- **1 can (about 15 ounces) chickpeas, undrained**
- **1 bay leaf**
- **⅛ teaspoon red pepper flakes**
- **1 cup uncooked orecchiette pasta**
- **Black pepper (optional)**
- **Chopped fresh parsley or basil (optional)**

1. Heat 3 tablespoons oil in large saucepan over medium-high heat. Add onion and carrot; cook 10 minutes or until vegetables are soft, stirring occasionally.
2. Add garlic, rosemary and 1 teaspoon salt; cook and stir 1 minute. Stir in tomatoes, broth, chickpeas with liquid, bay leaf and red pepper flakes. Remove 1 cup mixture to food processor or blender; process until smooth. Stir back into saucepan; bring to a boil.
3. Stir in pasta. Reduce heat to medium; cook 12 to 15 minutes or until pasta is tender. Remove and discard bay leaf and rosemary sprig. Taste and season with additional salt and black pepper, if desired. Garnish with parsley; drizzle with remaining 1 tablespoon oil.

Tip

To crush the tomatoes, take them out of the can one at a time and crush them between your fingers over the pot. Or coarsely chop them with a knife.

Italian Wedding Soup

Makes 8 servings

Meatballs

- 2 eggs
- 2 cloves garlic, minced
- 1 teaspoon salt
- ⅛ teaspoon black pepper
- 1½ pounds meat loaf mix (ground beef and pork)
- ¾ cup plain dry bread crumbs
- ½ cup grated Parmesan cheese
- 2 tablespoons olive oil

Soup

- 1 onion, chopped
- 2 carrots, chopped
- 4 cloves garlic, minced
- 2 heads escarole or curly endive, coarsely chopped
- 8 cups chicken broth
- 1 can (about 14 ounces) Italian plum tomatoes, undrained, coarsely chopped
- 3 sprigs fresh thyme
- 1 teaspoon salt
- ½ teaspoon red pepper flakes
- 1 cup uncooked acini di pepe pasta

1. For meatballs, whisk eggs, 2 cloves garlic, 1 teaspoon salt and black pepper in large bowl until blended. Stir in meat loaf mix, bread crumbs and cheese; mix gently until well blended. Shape mixture by tablespoonfuls into 1-inch balls.
2. Heat oil in large saucepan or Dutch oven over medium heat. Cook meatballs in batches 5 minutes or until browned. Remove to plate; set aside.
3. For soup, add onion, carrots and 4 cloves garlic to saucepan; cook and stir 5 minutes or until onion is lightly browned. Add escarole; cook and stir 2 minutes or until wilted. Stir in broth, tomatoes with juice, thyme, 1 teaspoon salt and red pepper flakes; bring to a boil over high heat. Reduce heat to medium-low; simmer, uncovered, 15 minutes.
4. Add meatballs and pasta to soup; return to a boil over high heat. Reduce heat to medium; cook 10 minutes or until pasta is tender, stirring occasionally. Remove and discard thyme sprigs before serving.

Japanese Noodle Soup

Makes 6 servings

- **1 package (8½ ounces) uncooked Japanese udon noodles**
- **1 tablespoon vegetable oil**
- **1 medium red bell pepper, cut into thin strips**
- **1 medium carrot, diagonally sliced**
- **2 green onions, thinly sliced**
- **2 cans (about 14 ounces each) beef broth**
- **1 cup water**
- **2 teaspoons soy sauce**
- **½ teaspoon grated fresh ginger**
- **½ teaspoon black pepper**
- **2 cups thinly sliced stemmed shiitake mushrooms**
- **4 ounces daikon (Japanese radish), peeled and cut into thin strips**
- **4 ounces firm tofu, drained and cut into ½-inch cubes**

1. Cook noodles according to package directions. Drain and rinse noodles; set aside.
2. Heat oil in large nonstick saucepan over medium-high heat. Add bell pepper, carrot and green onions; cook and stir about 3 minutes or until vegetables are slightly softened.
3. Stir in broth, water, soy sauce, ginger and black pepper; bring to a boil. Stir in mushrooms, daikon and tofu; cook over low heat 5 minutes.
4. Place noodles in serving bowls; ladle soup over noodles.

Hearty Vegetable Pasta Soup

Makes 6 servings

- **1 tablespoon vegetable oil**
- **1 onion, chopped**
- **3 cups vegetable broth**
- **1 can (about 14 ounces) diced tomatoes**
- **1 medium potato, peeled and cubed**
- **2 carrots, sliced**
- **1 stalk celery, sliced**
- **1 teaspoon dried basil**
- **½ teaspoon salt**
- **⅛ teaspoon black pepper**
- **⅓ cup uncooked mini bowtie pasta**
- **2 ounces fresh spinach, stemmed and chopped**

1. Heat oil in large saucepan or Dutch oven over medium-high heat. Add onion; cook and stir about 3 minutes or until translucent. Add broth, tomatoes, potato, carrots, celery, basil, salt and pepper; bring to a boil over high heat. Reduce heat to medium-low; simmer, uncovered, 20 minutes or until potato and carrots are very tender, stirring occasionally.
2. Stir in pasta; cook 8 minutes or until pasta is tender.
3. Stir in spinach; cook 2 minutes or until spinach is wilted. Serve immediately.

Rotini and Chickpea Chowder

Makes 6 servings

- 6 ounces uncooked rotini pasta
- 2 tablespoons olive oil
- ¾ cup chopped onion
- ½ cup thinly sliced carrot
- ½ cup chopped celery
- 2 cloves garlic, minced
- ¼ cup all-purpose flour
- 1½ teaspoons Italian seasoning
- ½ teaspoon salt
- ⅛ teaspoon red pepper flakes
- ⅛ teaspoon black pepper
- 2 cans (about 14 ounces each) chicken broth
- 1 can (about 15 ounces) chickpeas, rinsed and drained
- 1 can (about 14 ounces) Italian-style stewed tomatoes
- 6 slices bacon
- Grated Parmesan cheese

1. Cook pasta according to package directions; drain.
2. Meanwhile, heat oil in large saucepan or Dutch oven over medium heat. Add onion, carrot, celery and garlic; cook 5 minutes or until vegetables are crisp-tender, stirring frequently.
3. Remove from heat; stir in flour, Italian seasoning, salt, red pepper flakes and black pepper until well blended. Gradually add broth and return to a boil over high heat. Boil 1 minute, stirring constantly. Reduce heat to medium; stir in cooked pasta, chickpeas and tomatoes. Cook 5 minutes or until heated through.
4. Meanwhile, place bacon between double layer of paper towels on paper plate. Microwave on HIGH 5 to 6 minutes or until crisp. Drain on paper towel-lined plate; crumble into bite-size pieces.
5. Sprinkle soup with bacon and grated cheese. Serve immediately.

Pesto Tortellini Soup

Makes 6 servings

- **1 package (9 ounces) refrigerated cheese tortellini**
- **3 cans (about 14 ounces each) chicken or vegetable broth**
- **1 jar (7 ounces) roasted red peppers, drained and thinly sliced**
- **¾ cup frozen green peas**
- **3 to 4 cups packed stemmed fresh spinach**
- **2 tablespoons pesto sauce**
- **¼ teaspoon salt**
- **Grated Parmesan cheese (optional)**

1. Cook tortellini according to package directions; drain.
2. Bring broth to a boil in large saucepan or Dutch oven over high heat. Add cooked tortellini, roasted peppers and peas; return to a boil. Reduce heat to medium; cook 1 minute.
3. Remove from heat; stir in spinach, pesto and salt. Serve with cheese, if desired.

Tip

To easily remove stems from spinach leaves, fold each leaf in half, then pull the stem toward the top of the leaf.

Fresh Tomato Pasta Soup

Makes 8 servings

- 1 tablespoon olive oil
- ½ cup chopped onion
- 1 clove garlic, minced
- 3 pounds fresh tomatoes (about 9 medium), coarsely chopped
- 3 cups chicken broth
- 1 tablespoon minced fresh basil
- 1 tablespoon minced fresh oregano
- 1 teaspoon salt
- 1 teaspoon whole fennel seeds
- ½ teaspoon black pepper
- ¾ cup uncooked rosamarina, orzo or other small pasta
- ½ cup (2 ounces) shredded mozzarella cheese

1. Heat oil in large saucepan over medium heat. Add onion and garlic; cook and stir 4 minutes or until onion is tender.
2. Add tomatoes, broth, basil, oregano, salt, fennel seeds and pepper; bring to a boil. Reduce heat to low; cover and simmer 25 minutes. Remove from heat; cool slightly.
3. Blend tomato mixture in batches in blender or food processor until smooth. (Or use hand-held immersion blender.) Return soup to saucepan; bring to a boil.
4. Add pasta; cook 7 to 9 minutes or until tender, stirring frequently. Sprinkle with cheese.

Greek Lemon and Rice Soup

Makes 6 servings

- **2 tablespoons butter**
- **⅓ cup minced green onions**
- **6 cups chicken broth**
- **⅔ cup uncooked long grain rice**
- **4 eggs**
- **Juice of 1 lemon**
- **⅛ teaspoon black or white pepper (optional)**
- **Fresh mint sprigs and lemon peel (optional)**

1. Melt butter in medium saucepan over medium heat. Add green onions; cook and stir 3 minutes or until tender.
2. Stir in broth and rice; bring to a boil over medium-high heat. Reduce heat to low; cover and simmer 20 to 25 minutes or until rice is tender.
3. Beat eggs in medium bowl. Stir in lemon juice and ½ cup hot broth mixture until blended. Gradually pour egg mixture into broth mixture in saucepan, stirring constantly. Cook and stir over low heat 2 to 3 minutes or until soup thickens enough to lightly coat spoon. *Do not boil.*
4. Stir in pepper, if desired. Garnish with mint and lemon peel.

Matzo Ball Soup

Makes 6 servings

- 4 eggs
- 1 cup matzo meal
- ¼ cup (½ stick) butter or margarine, melted and cooled
- 2 tablespoons water
- 1 tablespoon grated onion
- ½ teaspoon salt
- ⅛ teaspoon white pepper *or* ¼ teaspoon black pepper
- 8 cups chicken broth
- Chopped fresh Italian parsley (optional)

1. Beat eggs in large bowl with electric mixer at medium speed. Add matzo meal, butter, 2 tablespoons water, onion, salt and pepper; beat at low speed until well blended. Let stand 15 to 30 minutes. With wet hands, shape mixture into 12 (2-inch) balls.
2. Bring 8 cups water to a boil in large saucepan or Dutch oven over medium-high heat. Drop matzo balls, one at a time, into boiling water. Reduce heat to low; cover and simmer 35 minutes or until cooked through. Remove matzo balls to plate; drain water.
3. Pour broth into same saucepan; bring to a boil over high heat. Add matzo balls. Reduce heat to low; cover and cook 5 minutes or until matzo balls are heated through. Garnish with parsley.

Pasta Meatball Soup

Makes 4 servings

- 10 ounces ground beef
- 5 tablespoons uncooked acini di pepe pasta,* divided
- ¼ cup fresh fine bread crumbs
- 1 egg
- 2 tablespoons finely chopped fresh parsley, divided
- 1 clove garlic, minced
- 1 teaspoon dried basil, divided
- ½ teaspoon salt
- ⅛ teaspoon black pepper
- 2 cans (about 14 ounces each) beef broth
- 1 can (about 8 ounces) tomato sauce
- ⅓ cup chopped onion

***Acini di pepe is tiny rice-shaped pasta. Orzo or pastina can be substituted.**

1. Combine beef, 2 tablespoons pasta, bread crumbs, egg, 1 tablespoon parsley, garlic, ½ teaspoon basil, salt and pepper in medium bowl; mix well Shape into 28 to 30 (1-inch) meatballs.
2. Combine broth, tomato sauce, onion and remaining ½ teaspoon basil to a boil in large saucepan; bring to a boil over medium-high heat. Carefully add meatballs to broth mixture. Reduce heat to medium-low; cover and simmer 20 minutes.
3. Stir in remaining 3 tablespoons pasta; cook 10 minutes or until pasta is tender. Garnish with remaining 1 tablespoon parsley.

Quick Vegetable Noodle Soup

Makes 4 servings

- **2 cans (about 14 ounces each) vegetable broth**
- **2 teaspoons minced garlic**
- **1 teaspoon minced fresh ginger**
- **¼ teaspoon red pepper flakes**
- **1 package (16 ounces) frozen vegetable medley, such as broccoli, carrots, water chestnuts and red bell peppers**
- **2 packages (3 ounces each) ramen noodles,* *or* 5 ounces uncooked angel hair pasta, broken in half**
- **3 tablespoons soy sauce**
- **1 tablespoon dark sesame oil**
- **¼ cup thinly sliced green onions**

Use any flavor; discard seasoning packets.

1 Combine broth, garlic, ginger and red pepper flakes in large saucepan; bring to a boil over high heat. Add vegetables and noodles; return to a boil. Reduce heat to medium-low; cook 5 to 6 minutes or until vegetables and noodles are tender, stirring occasionally.

2 Stir in soy sauce and sesame oil; cook 3 minutes. Stir in green onions just before serving.

Tip

For a heartier, protein-packed main dish, add 1 package (14 ounces) extra firm tofu, drained and cut into ¾-inch cubes, to the soup with the soy sauce and sesame oil.

Italian Fennel and Pasta Soup

Makes 4 servings

- **1 tablespoon olive oil**
- **1 small fennel bulb, trimmed and chopped into ¼-inch pieces (1½ cups)**
- **4 cloves garlic, minced**
- **3 cups vegetable broth**
- **1 cup uncooked small shell pasta**
- **½ teaspoon salt**
- **1 medium zucchini or yellow squash, cut into ½-inch pieces**
- **1 can (about 14 ounces) Italian-style diced tomatoes**
- **¼ cup grated Romano or Parmesan cheese**
- **¼ cup chopped fresh basil**
- **Black pepper**

1. Heat oil in large saucepan over medium heat. Add fennel; cook and stir 5 minutes. Add garlic; cook and stir 30 seconds. Add broth, pasta and salt; bring to a boil over high heat. Reduce heat to low; cook 5 minutes, stirring occasionally.
2. Stir in zucchini; cook 5 to 7 minutes or until pasta and vegetables are tender.
3. Stir in tomatoes; cook until heated through. Sprinkle with cheese, basil and pepper.

Beans & Legumes

French-Style Lentil Soup

Makes 4 to 6 servings

- 3 tablespoons olive oil
- 1 medium onion, chopped
- 1 carrot, chopped
- 1 stalk celery, chopped
- 1 clove garlic, minced
- 8 ounces dried lentils, rinsed and sorted
- 3 cups vegetable broth
- 1 can (about 14 ounces) stewed tomatoes
- 2 tablespoons balsamic vinegar
- ½ teaspoon salt
- Black pepper
- ½ cup grated Parmesan cheese (optional)

1. Heat oil in large saucepan over medium heat. Add onion, carrot, celery and garlic; cook 8 minutes or until vegetables are tender but not browned, stirring occasionally.
2. Stir in lentils, broth, tomatoes, vinegar and salt; bring to a boil over high heat. Reduce heat to low; cover and simmer 30 minutes or until lentils are tender.
3. Season with additional salt and pepper; sprinkle with cheese, if desired.

Fasolada (Greek White Bean Soup)

Makes 4 to 6 servings

- 4 tablespoons olive oil, divided
- 1 large onion, diced
- 3 stalks celery, diced
- 3 carrots, diced
- 4 cloves garlic, minced
- ¼ cup tomato paste
- 1 teaspoon salt
- 1 teaspoon dried oregano
- ½ teaspoon ground cumin
- ¼ teaspoon black pepper
- 1 bay leaf
- 4 cups vegetable broth
- 3 cans (15 ounces each) cannellini beans, rinsed and drained
- 2 tablespoons lemon juice
- ¼ cup minced fresh parsley

1. Heat 2 tablespoons oil in large saucepan or Dutch oven over medium-high heat. Add onion, celery and carrots; cook and stir 8 to 10 minutes or until vegetables are softened. Stir in garlic; cook and stir 30 seconds. Stir in tomato paste, salt, oregano, cumin, pepper and bay leaf; cook and stir 30 seconds.
2. Stir in broth; bring to a boil. Stir in beans; return to a boil. Reduce heat to medium-low; simmer, uncovered, 30 minutes.
3. Stir in remaining 2 tablespoons oil and lemon juice. Remove and discard bay leaf. Sprinkle with parsley just before serving.

Red Bean Soup

Makes 6 servings

- **1 pound dried red kidney beans, rinsed and sorted**
- **1 sprig fresh thyme, plus additional for garnish**
- **1 sprig fresh parsley**
- **2 tablespoons butter**
- **1 onion, finely chopped**
- **4 carrots, chopped**
- **2 stalks celery, chopped**
- **6 cups water**
- **1 pound smoked ham hocks**
- **3 cloves garlic, minced**
- **1 bay leaf**
- **½ teaspoon salt**
- **¼ teaspoon black pepper**
- **2 tablespoons lemon juice**
- **Sour cream (optional)**

1. Place beans in large bowl; cover with water and soak 6 to 8 hours or overnight.
2. Drain and rinse beans. Tie together thyme and parsley sprigs with kitchen string.
3. Melt butter in large saucepan or Dutch oven over medium-high heat. Add onion; cook and stir 3 minutes or until softened. Add carrots and celery; cook and stir 5 minutes or until vegetables begin to brown. Add 6 cups water, beans, ham hocks, garlic, bay leaf and fresh herb sprigs; bring to a boil over high heat. Reduce heat to low; cover and simmer 1 hour 30 minutes or until beans are softened. Remove and discard ham hocks, herb sprigs and bay leaf. Stir in salt and pepper.
4. Blend soup in batches in blender or food processor until smooth. (Or use hand-held immersion blender.) Return soup to saucepan; bring to a simmer. Stir in lemon juice; season with additional salt and pepper. Serve with sour cream, if desired; garnish with additional fresh thyme.

Black Bean Soup

Substitute dried black beans for the red kidney beans. Proceed as directed, simmering soup 1½ to 2 hours or until beans are tender. Add 4 to 5 tablespoons dry sherry instead of lemon juice.

Cranberry Bean Soup

Substitute dried cranberry beans for the red kidney beans. Proceed as directed, simmering soup 2 to 2¼ hours or until beans are tender.

Ribollita (Tuscan Bread Soup)

Makes 6 servings

- 2 tablespoons olive oil
- 1 onion, halved and thinly sliced
- 2 stalks celery, diced
- 1 large carrot, julienned
- 2 medium zucchini, halved lengthwise and thinly sliced
- 1 medium yellow squash, halved lengthwise and thinly sliced
- 3 cloves garlic, minced
- 1 can (about 28 ounces) whole tomatoes, undrained
- 1 can (15 ounces) cannellini beans, rinsed and drained
- 1½ teaspoons salt
- 1 teaspoon dried Italian seasoning
- ¼ teaspoon black pepper
- 1 bay leaf
- ¼ teaspoon red pepper flakes (optional)
- 4 cups vegetable broth
- 2 cups water
- 1 bunch kale, stemmed and coarsely chopped *or* 3 cups thinly sliced cabbage
- 8 ounces Tuscan or other rustic bread, cubed
- Shredded Parmesan cheese (optional)

1. Heat oil in large saucepan or Dutch oven over medium-high heat. Add onion, celery and carrot; cook and stir 5 minutes. Add zucchini, yellow squash and garlic; cook and stir 5 minutes.
2. Add tomatoes with juice, beans, salt, Italian seasoning, black pepper, bay leaf and red pepper flakes, if desired. Stir in broth and water; bring to a boil. Reduce heat to low; simmer, uncovered, 15 minutes.
3. Stir in kale and bread; cook 10 minutes or until vegetables are tender and soup is thick. Serve with cheese, if desired.

Note

This recipe is a great way to use up stale or day-old bread. Cut the bread into cubes ahead of time and leave it out at room temperature for several hours. Or spread bread cubes on a baking sheet and bake at 350°F until the bread is dry but not browned.

Greens, White Bean and Barley Soup

Makes 6 to 8 servings

- 2 tablespoons olive oil
- 1½ cups chopped onions
- 3 carrots, diced
- 2 cloves garlic, minced
- 1½ cups sliced mushrooms
- 6 cups vegetable broth
- 2 cups cooked barley
- 1 can (about 15 ounces) Great Northern beans, rinsed and drained
- 1 teaspoon sugar
- 1 teaspoon dried thyme
- 2 bay leaves
- ½ teaspoon salt
- 7 cups chopped stemmed collard greens (about 1½ pounds)
- 1 tablespoon white wine vinegar
- Hot pepper sauce
- Red bell pepper strips (optional)

1. Heat oil in large saucepan or Dutch oven over medium heat. Add onions, carrots and garlic; cook and stir 3 minutes. Add mushrooms; cook and stir 5 minutes or until carrots are tender.

2. Add broth, barley, beans, sugar, thyme, bay leaves and salt; bring to a boil over high heat. Reduce heat to medium-low; cover and simmer 5 minutes.

3. Add greens; cook 10 minutes, stirring occasionally. Remove and discard bay leaves. Stir in vinegar and hot pepper sauce. Garnish with red bell pepper.

Groundnut Soup with Ginger and Cilantro

Makes 4 servings

- 1 tablespoon vegetable oil
- 1½ cups chopped onion
- 1 clove garlic, minced
- 2 teaspoons chili powder
- 1 teaspoon ground cumin
- ¼ teaspoon red pepper flakes
- 3 cups vegetable broth
- 1 can (about 14 ounces) diced tomatoes,
- 8 ounces sweet potatoes, peeled and cut into ½-inch pieces
- 1 medium carrot, cut into ½-inch pieces
- 1 cup salted peanuts
- 1 tablespoon grated fresh ginger
- ¼ cup chopped fresh cilantro

1. Heat oil in large saucepan over medium-high heat. Add onion; cook and stir 4 minutes or until translucent. Add garlic, chili powder, cumin and red pepper flakes; cook and stir 15 seconds.
2. Add broth, tomatoes, sweet potatoes and carrot; bring to a boil over high heat. Reduce heat to medium; cover and cook 25 minutes or until vegetables are tender, stirring occasionally. Remove from heat; stir in peanuts and ginger. Cool slightly.
3. Blend soup in batches in blender or food processor until smooth. (Or use hand-held immersion blender.) Return soup to saucepan; heat over medium-high heat 2 minutes or until heated through. Sprinkle with cilantro.

Italian-Style Bean Soup

Makes 8 to 10 servings

- **1½ cups dried Great Northern or navy beans, rinsed and sorted**
- **6 cups water**
- **1 cup pasta sauce**
- **1 tablespoon dried minced onion**
- **2 teaspoons dried basil**
- **2 cubes chicken bouillon**
- **1 teaspoon dried parsley flakes**
- **½ teaspoon minced garlic**
- **1½ cups uncooked medium pasta shells**
- **8 ounces baby spinach (optional)**
- **Salt and black pepper**
- **¼ cup grated Parmesan cheese**

1. Place beans in large bowl; cover with water and soak 6 to 8 hours or overnight.*
2. Drain and rinse beans. Combine beans, 6 cups water, pasta sauce, onion, basil, bouillon, parsley flakes and garlic in large saucepan or Dutch oven; bring to a boil over high heat. Reduce heat to low; cover and simmer 2 to 2½ hours.
3. Stir in pasta and spinach, if desired; cover and cook 15 to 20 minutes or until pasta is tender. Season with salt and pepper. Top with cheese.

**To quick-soak beans, place in large saucepan and cover with water. Bring to a boil over high heat; boil 2 minutes. Remove from heat; let stand, covered, 1 hour. Drain and proceed as directed.*

Classic Lentil Soup

Makes 6 to 8 servings

- 2 tablespoons olive oil, divided
- 2 medium onions, chopped
- 1½ teaspoons salt
- 4 cloves garlic, minced
- ¼ cup tomato paste
- 1 teaspoon dried oregano
- ½ teaspoon dried basil
- ¼ teaspoon dried thyme
- ¼ teaspoon black pepper
- ½ cup dry sherry or white wine
- 8 cups vegetable broth
- 2 cups water
- 3 carrots, cut into ½-inch pieces
- 2 cups dried lentils, rinsed and sorted
- 1 cup chopped fresh parsley
- 1 tablespoon balsamic vinegar

1. Heat 1 tablespoon oil in large saucepan or Dutch oven over medium heat. Add onions; cook 10 minutes, stirring occasionally. Add remaining 1 tablespoon oil and salt; cook 10 minutes or until onions are golden brown, stirring frequently.
2. Add garlic; cook and stir 1 minute. Add tomato paste, oregano, basil, thyme and pepper; cook and stir 1 minute. Stir in sherry; cook 30 seconds, scraping up browned bits from bottom of saucepan.
3. Stir in broth, water, carrots and lentils; cover and bring to a boil over high heat. Reduce heat to medium-low; cook, partially covered, 30 minutes or until lentils are tender.
4. Remove from heat; stir in parsley and vinegar.

Bean Soup Provençale

Makes 8 to 10 servings

- **Pesto Sauce (recipe follows)**
- **¼ cup vegetable oil**
- **1½ cups chopped onions**
- **1½ cups chopped celery**
- **1 cup sliced leeks**
- **8 cups water**
- **1 cup sliced carrots**
- **1 turnip, peeled and diced**
- **1 teaspoon salt**
- **¼ teaspoon black pepper**
- **2 cans (about 15 ounces each) Great Northern beans, rinsed and drained**
- **1 small zucchini, sliced**
- **1 cup fresh or frozen chopped spinach**

1 Prepare Pesto Sauce; set aside.

2 Heat oil in large saucepan over medium heat. Add onions, celery and leeks; cook 10 minutes or until onion is soft, stirring frequently.

3 Stir in water, carrots, turnip, salt and pepper; bring to a boil over high heat. Reduce heat to low; cover and simmer 30 minutes or until vegeteables are tender.

4 Add beans, zucchini and spinach; cook until heated through. Top with pesto.

Pesto Sauce

Combine ½ cup chopped fresh parsley, ¼ cup grated Parmesan cheese, ¼ cup olive oil, 1 tablespoon dried basil, 2 cloves garlic and 1 teaspoon lemon juice in food processor or blender; process until smooth.

Navy Bean Vegetable Soup
with Tortilla Strips

Makes 8 servings

- **1 cup dried navy beans, rinsed and sorted**
- **3 cups water**
- **1½ teaspoons salt, divided**
- **6 cups vegetable broth**
- **1 pound leeks (about 2), cut into ½-inch pieces**
- **12 ounces new potatoes or small red potatoes, halved**
- **2 cups sliced mushrooms**
- **1½ cups thinly sliced carrots**
- **1½ teaspoons dried thyme**
- **1 bay leaf**
- **½ teaspoon black pepper**
- **2 (6-inch) corn tortillas**
- **2 teaspoons olive oil**
- **¼ teaspoon garlic salt**
- **1 cup diced fresh tomato (optional)**

1. Combine beans and water in large saucepan or Dutch oven; bring to a boil over high heat. Remove from heat; cover and let stand 30 minutes.
2. Return to a boil over high heat. Reduce heat to low; cover and simmer 30 minutes. Stir in ½ teaspoon salt; cover and simmer 1 hour. Drain beans; set aside.
3. Add broth, leeks, potatoes, mushrooms, carrots, thyme, bay leaf, remaining 1 teaspoon salt and pepper to same saucepan; bring to a boil over high heat. Reduce heat to low; cover and simmer 25 minutes. Stir in beans; cook 5 minutes or until heated through. Remove and discard bay leaf.
4. While soup is cooking, prepare tortilla strips. Preheat oven to 425°F. Brush both sides of tortillas lightly with oil; sprinkle one side of tortillas with garlic salt. Cut into ¼-inch strips. Arrange in single layer on baking sheet; bake 5 to 6 minutes or until crisp. Cool to room temperature.
5. Serve soup topped with chopped tomato, if desired, and tortilla strips.

West African Peanut Soup

Makes 6 to 8 servings

- 2 tablespoons vegetable oil
- 1 large onion, chopped
- ½ cup chopped roasted peanuts
- 1½ tablespoons minced fresh ginger
- 4 cloves garlic, minced (about 1 tablespoon)
- 1 teaspoon salt
- 4 cups vegetable broth
- 2 sweet potatoes, peeled and cut into ½-inch cubes
- 1 can (28 ounces) whole tomatoes, drained and coarsely chopped
- ¼ teaspoon ground red pepper
- 1 bunch Swiss chard or kale, stemmed and shredded
- ⅓ cup unsweetened peanut butter (creamy or chunky)

1. Heat oil in large saucepan or Dutch oven over medium-high heat. Add onion; cook and stir 5 minutes or until softened. Add peanuts, ginger, garlic and salt; cook and stir 1 minute. Stir in broth, sweet potatoes, tomatoes and red pepper; bring to a boil. Reduce heat to medium; cook 10 minutes.
2. Stir in chard and peanut butter; cook over medium-low heat 10 minutes or until vegetables are tender and soup is creamy.

Kale and White Bean Soup

Makes 4 servings

- **2 slices bacon, chopped**
- **½ cup diced onion**
- **1 large unpeeled new red potato, diced**
- **2 cans (about 14 ounces each) vegetable broth**
- **1 teaspoon minced garlic**
- **½ teaspoon salt**
- **½ teaspoon dried oregano**
- **¼ teaspoon black pepper**
- **2 bay leaves**
- **1 can (14½ ounces) sliced carrots, drained**
- **1 can (13½ ounces) kale or spinach, drained**
- **1 can (10 ounces) cannellini or Great Northern beans, rinsed and drained**
- **⅓ cup finely chopped oil-packed sun-dried tomatoes**

1. Cook bacon in large saucepan over medium heat until crisp.
2. Add onion and potato; cook and stir 10 minutes or until onion is lightly browned, stirring occasionally.
3. Stir in broth, garlic, salt, oregano, pepper and bay leaves; bring to a simmer. Reduce heat to medium-low; cover and cook 5 minutes or until potato is tender.
4. Stir in carrots, kale, beans and sun-dried tomatoes; cook 5 minutes. Remove and discard bay leaves.

Curried Coconut Lentil Soup

Makes 4 servings

- 1 tablespoon vegetable oil
- 1½ cups dried red lentils, rinsed and sorted
- ¼ cup minced onion
- ¼ cup unsweetened shredded coconut, plus additional for garnish
- 3 tablespoons curry powder
- 2 tablespoons chopped fresh parsley
- 1 teaspoon ground ginger
- ½ teaspoon garlic powder
- ½ teaspoon salt
- ½ teaspoon black pepper
- 1 container (48 ounces) vegetable broth
- 2 cups water

1. Heat oil in large saucepan over medium heat. Add lentils, onion, ¼ cup coconut, curry powder, parsley, ginger, garlic powder, salt and pepper; cook and stir 1 minute or until spices are fragrant.
2. Stir in broth and water; bring to a boil over high heat. Reduce heat to low; simmer, uncovered, 20 minutes or until lentils are tender. Garnish with additional coconut.

Smoky Vegetable Bean Soup

Makes 4 servings

- **2 tablespoons olive oil, divided**
- **1 medium orange, red or yellow bell pepper, chopped**
- **1 clove garlic, minced**
- **2 cups water**
- **1 can (about 14 ounces) diced tomatoes**
- **1 medium zucchini, thinly sliced lengthwise**
- **1 teaspoon salt**
- **⅛ teaspoon red pepper flakes**
- **1 can (about 15 ounces) navy or cannellini beans, rinsed and drained**
- **3 to 4 tablespoons chopped fresh basil**
- **1 tablespoon balsamic vinegar**
- **½ teaspoon liquid smoke**

1. Heat 1 tablespoon oil in large saucepan or Dutch oven over medium-high heat. Add bell pepper; cook and stir 4 minutes or until edges begin to brown. Add garlic; cook and stir 15 seconds.

2. Stir in water, tomatoes, zucchini, salt and red pepper flakes; bring to a boil over high heat. Reduce heat to low; cover and simmer 20 minutes.

3. Stir in beans, basil, remaining 1 tablespoon oil, vinegar and liquid smoke; cook 5 minutes. Remove from heat; let stand, covered, 10 minutes before serving.

Vegetables

Coconut Cauliflower Cream Soup

Makes 6 servings

- 1 tablespoon coconut or vegetable oil
- 1 medium onion, chopped
- 1 tablespoon minced garlic
- 1 tablespoon minced fresh ginger
- 1 teaspoon salt
- 1 head cauliflower (1½ pounds), cut into florets
- 2 cans (about 13 ounces each) coconut milk, divided
- 1 cup water
- 1 teaspoon garam masala
- ½ teaspoon ground turmeric
- Optional toppings: hot chili oil, smoked paprika, chopped fresh cilantro

1. Heat oil in large saucepan over medium-high heat. Add onion; cook and stir 5 minutes or until softened. Add garlic, ginger and salt; cook and stir 30 seconds.
2. Stir in cauliflower, 1 can coconut milk, water, garam masala and turmeric. Reduce heat to medium; cover and simmer 20 minutes or until cauliflower is very tender.
3. Remove from heat; blend soup with immersion blender until smooth.*
4. Return saucepan to medium heat. Add 1 cup coconut milk; cook and stir until heated through. Add additional coconut milk, if desired, to reach desired consistency. Top as desired.

**Or blend soup in batches with blender or food processor. Cool slightly before transferring to blender.*

Summer Corn Chowder

Makes 6 servings

- **5 ears corn, shucked**
- **2 tablespoons butter**
- **1 medium onion, chopped**
- **1 large poblano pepper, diced (¼-inch pieces)**
- **2 cloves garlic, minced**
- **1 container (32 ounces) chicken or vegetable broth**
- **1½ teaspoons salt, divided**
- **½ teaspoon black pepper, divided**
- **¼ teaspoon ground red pepper**
- **1 pound red potatoes, peeled and cut into ½-inch pieces**
- **3 plum tomatoes, diced (about 2 cups)**
- **½ cup whipping cream**
- **2 tablespoons lime juice**
- **2 tablespoons chopped fresh cilantro**
- **¼ cup crumbled crisp-cooked bacon (optional)**

1. Cut kernels off cobs; place in medium bowl. Working over bowl, run back of knife up and down cobs to release additional corn pulp and milk from cobs into bowl. Break cobs in half; set aside.
2. Melt butter in large saucepan or Dutch oven over medium heat. Add onion, poblano pepper and garlic; cook 5 minutes or until vegetables are softened, stirring occasionally. Stir in broth, 1 teaspoon salt, ¼ teaspoon black pepper and red pepper; mix well. Add corn cobs; bring to a boil. Reduce heat to medium-low; cover and simmer 15 minutes.
3. Stir in potatoes; cover and cook 20 minutes. Stir in corn kernels and tomatoes; cook, uncovered, 20 minutes. Remove and discard corn cobs. Coarsely mash soup with potato masher. (Or use hand-held immersion blender to briefly blend soup just until slightly chunky.)
4. Stir in cream; cook 3 minutes or until heated through. Stir in lime juice, cilantro, remaining ½ teaspoon salt and ¼ teaspoon black pepper. Garnish with bacon.

Garden Vegetable Soup

Makes 8 to 10 servings

- 1 tablespoon olive oil
- 1 medium onion, chopped
- 1 carrot, chopped
- 1 stalk celery, chopped
- 1 medium zucchini, diced
- 1 medium yellow squash, diced
- 1 red bell pepper, diced
- 2 tablespoons tomato paste
- 2 cloves garlic, minced
- 2 teaspoons salt
- 1 teaspoon Italian seasoning
- ½ teaspoon black pepper
- 8 cups vegetable broth
- 1 can (28 ounces) whole tomatoes, undrained, chopped
- ½ cup uncooked pearl barley
- 1 cup cut green beans (1-inch pieces)
- ½ cup corn
- ¼ cup slivered fresh basil
- 1 tablespoon lemon juice

1. Heat oil in large saucepan or Dutch oven over medium-high heat. Add onion, carrot and celery; cook and stir 8 minutes or until vegetables are softened. Add zucchini, yellow squash and bell pepper; cook and stir 5 minutes or until softened.
2. Add tomato paste, garlic, salt, Italian seasoning and black pepper; cook and stir 1 minute. Stir in broth and tomatoes with juice; bring to a boil. Stir in barley. Reduce heat to low; simmer, uncovered, 30 minutes.
3. Stir in green beans and corn; cook 15 minutes or until barley is tender and beans are crisp-tender. Stir in basil and lemon juice.

Harvest Pumpkin Soup

Makes 8 servings

- 1 sugar pumpkin or acorn squash (about 2 pounds)
- 1 kabocha or butternut squash (about 2 pounds)
- Salt and black pepper
- 2 tablespoons olive oil
- 2 tablespoons butter
- 1 large onion, finely chopped
- 2 stalks celery, chopped
- 1 medium carrot, chopped
- ¼ cup packed brown sugar
- 2 tablespoons tomato paste
- 1 tablespoon minced fresh ginger
- 1 clove garlic, minced
- 1 teaspoon salt
- 1 teaspoon ground cinnamon
- ¼ teaspoon ground cumin
- ¼ teaspoon black pepper
- 4 cups vegetable broth
- 1 cup milk
- 2 teaspoons lemon juice
- Roasted pumpkin seeds (optional, see Tip)

1. Preheat oven to 400°F. Line large baking sheet with foil; spray with nonstick cooking spray.
2. Cut pumpkin and kabocha squash in half; remove and discard seeds and strings or reserve seeds to roast (see Tip). Season cut sides with salt and pepper. Place squash cut sides down on prepared baking sheet; bake 30 to 45 minutes or until fork-tender. When squash is cool enough to handle, remove skin; chop flesh into 1-inch pieces.
3. Heat oil and butter in large saucepan or Dutch oven over medium-high heat. Add onion, celery and carrot; cook and stir 5 minutes or until vegetables are tender. Add brown sugar, tomato paste, ginger, garlic, 1 teaspoon salt, cinnamon, cumin and ¼ teaspoon pepper; cook and stir 1 minute. Stir in broth and squash; bring to a boil. Reduce heat to medium; simmer, uncovered, 20 minutes or until squash is very soft.
4. Blend soup with hand-held immersion blender until desired consistency. (Or blend soup in batches in blender or food processor.) Stir in milk and lemon juice; cook until heated through. Garnish with pumpkin seeds.

Tip

Roasted pumpkin seeds can be found at many supermarkets, or you can roast the seeds that you remove from the pumpkin (and the squash) in the recipe. Combine the seeds with ½ teaspoon vegetable oil and ⅛ teaspoon salt in a small bowl; toss to coat. Spread on a small foil-lined baking sheet; bake at 300°F about 20 minutes or until the seeds begin to brown, stirring once.

Cream of Asparagus Soup

Makes 6 to 8 servings

- **1 pound asparagus**
- **3½ cups vegetable or chicken broth, divided**
- **¼ cup (½ stick) butter**
- **¼ cup all-purpose flour**
- **½ cup whipping cream**
- **½ teaspoon salt**
- **⅛ teaspoon black pepper**

1. Trim off and discard tough ends of asparagus. Cut asparagus into 1-inch pieces. Combine asparagus and 1 cup broth in medium saucepan; cook over medium heat 12 to 15 minutes or until tender.
2. Remove 1 cup asparagus pieces to small bowl. Transfer remaining asparagus pieces and broth to blender or food processor; blend until smooth. (Or use hand-held immersion blender.)
3. Melt butter in large saucepan over medium heat. Stir in flour until smooth. Gradually add remaining 2½ cups broth; cook until slightly thickened, stirring occasionally. Stir in cream, salt, pepper, puréed asparagus and reserved asparagus pieces; cook and stir until heated through.

Oven-Roasted Onion Soup

Makes 4 servings

- ¼ cup (½ stick) butter
- 3 yellow onions, thinly sliced
- 1 teaspoon salt
- ½ teaspoon ground pepper
- 6 cups reduced-sodium beef broth
- ½ cup brewed coffee
- ¼ cup dry sherry
- 1 small baguette, cut into ½-inch slices
- 1 cup grated Swiss cheese
- 6 small sprigs thyme (optional)

1. Preheat oven to 325°F. Melt butter in Dutch oven over medium heat. Add onions, salt and pepper; cook 15 minutes or until onions are golden brown, stirring occasionally. Cover and bake 45 minutes, stirring once.
2. Stir in broth; cover and bake 30 minutes. Return soup to stovetop; stir in coffee and sherry. Bring to a simmer over medium heat.
3. Meanwhile, place baguette slices on baking sheet. Bake until lightly browned on both sides, turning once. *Turn oven to broil.*
4. Ladle soup into four ovenproof bowls; top each serving with two toasted baguette slices and 1 tablespoon cheese. Place bowls on baking sheet; broil 2 to 3 minutes or until cheese is melted and bubbly. Garnish with thyme.

Broccoli Cheese Soup

Makes 4 to 6 servings

- 6 tablespoons (¾ stick) butter
- 1 cup chopped onion
- 1 clove garlic, minced
- ¼ cup all-purpose flour
- 2 cups vegetable broth
- 2 cups milk
- 1½ teaspoons Dijon mustard
- ½ teaspoon salt
- ¼ teaspoon ground nutmeg
- ¼ teaspoon black pepper
- ⅛ teaspoon hot pepper sauce
- 1 package (16 ounces) frozen broccoli (5 cups)
- 2 carrots, shredded (1 cup)
- 6 ounces pasteurized process cheese product, cubed
- 1 cup (4 ounces) shredded sharp Cheddar cheese, plus additional for garnish

1. Melt butter in large saucepan or Dutch oven over medium-low heat. Add onion; cook and stir 8 minutes or until softened. Add garlic; cook and stir 1 minute. Increase heat to medium. Whisk in flour until smooth; cook and stir 3 minutes without browning.
2. Gradually whisk in broth and milk. Add mustard, salt, nutmeg, black pepper and hot pepper sauce; cook 15 minutes or until thickened, stirring occasionally.
3. Add broccoli; cook 15 minutes. Add carrots; cook 10 minutes or until vegetables are tender.
4. Remove half of soup to food processor or blender; process until smooth. Return to saucepan. Add cheese product and 1 cup Cheddar; cook and stir over low heat until cheese is melted. Garnish soup with additional Cheddar.

Italian Mushroom Soup

Makes 6 to 8 servings

- ½ cup dried porcini mushrooms (about ½ ounce)
- 1 tablespoon olive oil
- 2 cups chopped onions
- 8 ounces sliced cremini or button mushrooms
- 2 cloves garlic, minced
- ½ teaspoon salt
- ¼ teaspoon dried thyme
- ¼ cup all-purpose flour
- 4 cups vegetable broth
- ½ cup whipping cream
- ⅓ cup Marsala wine (optional)
- Black pepper

1. Place dried mushrooms in small bowl; cover with boiling water. Let stand 15 minutes or until softened.
2. Meanwhile, heat oil in large saucepan over medium heat. Add onions; cook 5 minutes or until translucent, stirring occasionally. Add cremini mushrooms, garlic, salt and thyme; cook 8 minutes or until softened, stirring occasionally. If desired, remove several mushrooms for garnish and set aside. Add flour; cook and stir 1 minute. Stir in broth.
3. Drain porcini mushrooms, reserving soaking liquid. Chop mushrooms; add to saucepan with reserved liquid. Bring to a boil. Reduce heat to medium-low; simmer, uncovered, 10 minutes. Cool slightly.
4. Blend soup in batches in blender or food processor until smooth. (Or use hand-held immersion blender.) Return soup to saucepan over medium-low heat. Stir in cream and Marsala, if desired; season with additional salt and pepper. Cook 5 minutes or until heated through. Garnish with reserved mushrooms.

Two-Cheese Potato and Cauliflower Soup

Makes 4 to 6 servings

- **1 tablespoon butter**
- **1 cup chopped onion**
- **2 cloves garlic, minced**
- **5 cups whole milk**
- **1 pound Yukon Gold potatoes, peeled and diced**
- **1 pound cauliflower florets**
- **1½ teaspoons salt**
- **⅛ teaspoon ground red pepper**
- **1½ cups (6 ounces) shredded sharp Cheddar cheese**
- **⅓ cup crumbled blue cheese**

1. Melt butter in large saucepan over medium-high heat. Add onion; cook and stir 4 minutes or until translucent. Add garlic; cook and stir 15 seconds. Stir in milk, potatoes, cauliflower, salt and red pepper; bring to a boil. Reduce heat to low; cover and simmer 15 minutes or until potatoes are tender. Cool slightly.
2. Working in batches, blend soup in blender or food processor until smooth. (Or use hand-held immersion blender.) Return soup to saucepan; cook over medium heat just until heated through.
3. Remove from heat; stir in Cheddar and blue cheese until melted.

Tip

One pound of trimmed cauliflower will yield about 1½ cups of florets. You can also substitute 1 pound of frozen cauliflower florets for the fresh florets.

Creamy Roasted Poblano Soup

Makes 4 servings

- 6 large poblano peppers
- 1 tablespoon olive oil
- ¾ cup chopped onion
- ½ cup thinly sliced celery
- ½ cup thinly sliced carrots
- 1 clove garlic, minced
- 2 cans (about 14 ounces each) vegetable broth
- ½ teaspoon salt
- 1 package (8 ounces) cream cheese, cubed
- Black pepper

1. Preheat broiler. Line broiler pan or baking sheet with foil. Place poblano peppers in pan; broil 5 to 6 inches from heat source 15 minutes or until peppers are blistered and beginning to char, turning occasionally. Place peppers in medium bowl; cover with plastic wrap. Let stand 20 minutes.
2. Meanwhile, heat oil in large saucepan over medium-high heat. Add onion, celery, carrots and garlic; cook and stir 4 minutes or until onion is translucent. Stir in broth and salt; bring to a boil. Reduce heat to medium-low; cover and simmer 12 minutes or until celery is tender.
3. Remove skins, stems and seeds from peppers. Briefly run peppers under cold water to help remove skins and seeds, if necessary. (This removes some smoky flavor, so work quickly.) Add peppers to broth mixture.
4. Working in batches, blend broth mixture and cream cheese in blender or food processor until smooth. (Or use hand-held immersion blender.) Return soup to saucepan; cook and stir over medium heat 2 minutes or until heated through. Season with additional salt and black pepper.

Curried Parsnip Soup

Makes 6 to 8 servings

- 3 pounds parsnips, peeled and cut into 2-inch pieces
- 1 tablespoon olive oil
- 2 tablespoons butter
- 1 medium yellow onion, chopped
- 2 stalks celery, diced
- 1 tablespoon salt
- 3 cloves garlic, minced
- 1 to 2 teaspoons curry powder
- ½ teaspoon grated fresh ginger
- ½ teaspoon black pepper
- 8 cups reduced-sodium chicken broth
- Toasted bread slices (optional)
- Chopped fresh chives (optional)

1. Preheat oven to 400°F. Line baking sheet with foil.
2. Combine parsnips and oil in large bowl; toss to coat. Spread in single layer on prepared baking sheet. Bake 35 to 45 minutes or until parsnips are tender and lightly browned around edges, stirring once halfway through cooking.
3. Melt butter in large saucepan or Dutch oven over medium heat. Add onion and celery; cook and stir about 8 minutes or until vegetables are tender and onion is translucent. Add salt, garlic, curry powder, ginger and pepper; cook and stir 1 minute. Add parsnips and broth; bring to a boil over medium-high heat. Reduce heat to medium-low; cover and simmer 10 minutes.
4. Working in batches, blend soup in blender or food processor until smooth. (Or use hand-held immersion blender.) Serve with toasted bread, if desired; garnish with chives.

Perfect Tomato Soup

Makes 6 servings

- **1 tablespoon vegetable oil**
- **1 cup chopped onion**
- **2 cloves garlic, coarsely chopped**
- **½ cup chopped carrot**
- **¼ cup chopped celery**
- **2 cans (28 ounces each) crushed tomatoes**
- **3½ cups chicken broth**
- **1 tablespoon Worcestershire sauce**
- **1 teaspoon salt**
- **½ teaspoon dried thyme**
- **¼ to ½ teaspoon black pepper**
- **2 to 4 drops hot pepper sauce**

1. Heat oil in large saucepan or Dutch oven over medium-high heat. Add onion and garlic; cook and stir 3 minutes or until softened. Add carrot and celery; cook 7 minutes or until vegetables are tender, stirring frequently.
2. Stir in tomatoes, broth, Worcestershire sauce, salt, thyme, black pepper and hot pepper sauce; bring to a boil. Reduce heat to low; cover and simmer 20 minutes, stirring occasionallly.
3. For smoother soup, use hand-held immersion blender to blend until smooth. (Or blend soup in batches in in food processor or blender.)

Potato Soup with Chiles and Cheese

Makes 4 to 6 servings

- **2 tablespoons vegetable oil**
- **1 medium onion, chopped**
- **1 clove garlic, minced**
- **2 cups chopped unpeeled potatoes**
- **1 tablespoon all-purpose flour**
- **1½ cups chicken broth**
- **½ teaspoon salt**
- **2 cups milk**
- **1 can (4 ounces) diced green chiles, drained**
- **½ teaspoon celery salt**
- **¾ cup (3 ounces) shredded Monterey Jack cheese**
- **¾ cup (3 ounces) shredded Colby or Cheddar cheese**
- **White pepper**

1. Heat oil in large saucepan over medium-high heat. Add onion and garlic; cook and stir 4 minutes or until onion is tender. Add potatoes; cook and stir 1 minute. Add flour; cook and stir 1 minute.
2. Stir in broth and salt; bring to a boil. Reduce heat to medium-low; cover and simmer 20 minutes or until potatoes are tender.
3. Stir in milk, chiles and celery salt; cook 5 minutes. Add Monterey Jack and Cheddar; cook and stir just until cheese is melted. *Do not boil.* Season with additional salt and white pepper.

Cream of Broccoli Soup with Croutons

Makes 8 servings

- **3 cups French or rustic Italian bread cubes (½-inch cubes)**
- **1 tablespoon butter, melted**
- **1 tablespoon olive oil**
- **¼ cup grated Parmesan cheese**
- **2 tablespoons butter**
- **1 large onion, chopped**
- **8 cups (about 1½ pounds) chopped broccoli**
- **3 cups chicken broth**
- **1 cup whipping cream or half-and-half**
- **1½ teaspoons salt**
- **½ teaspoon black pepper**

1. Preheat oven to 350°F. Line baking sheet with parchment paper or foil.
2. Combine bread cubes, 1 tablespoon melted butter and oil in large bowl; toss to coat. Add cheese; toss again. Spread bread cubes in single layer on prepared baking sheet.
3. Bake 12 to 14 minutes or until golden brown, stirring after 8 minutes. Cool completely; remove to airtight container. (Croutons may be prepared up to 2 days before serving.)
4. Melt 2 tablespoons butter in large saucepan or Dutch oven over medium heat. Add onion; cook 5 minutes, stirring occasionally. Add broccoli and broth; bring to a boil over high heat. Reduce heat to low; simmer, uncovered, 25 minutes or until broccoli is very tender. Cool 10 minutes.
5. Blend soup in batches in blender or food processor until smooth. (Or use hand-held immersion blender.) Return soup to saucepan; stir in cream, salt and pepper. Cook over medium heat until heated through. *Do not boil.* Top with croutons.

Curried Sweet Potato Soup

Makes 4 servings

- **4 cups water**
- **1 pound sweet potatoes, peeled and cut into 1-inch pieces**
- **2 tablespoons butter, divided**
- **2 cups finely chopped yellow onions**
- **2 cups milk, divided**
- **¾ teaspoon curry powder**
- **½ teaspoon salt**
- **Dash ground red pepper (optional)**

1 Bring water to a boil in large saucepan over high heat. Add sweet potatoes; return to a boil. Reduce heat to medium-low; simmer, uncovered, 15 minutes or until sweet potatoes are tender.

2 Meanwhile, melt 1 tablespoon butter in large skillet over medium-high heat. Add onions; cook 10 minutes or until tender and golden brown, stirring occasionally.

3 Drain sweet potatoes; transfer to blender. Add cooked onions, 1 cup milk, curry powder, salt and red pepper, if desired; blend until smooth.

4 Return sweet potato mixture to saucepan over medium-high heat. Stir in remaining 1 cup milk; cook 5 minutes or until heated through, stirring frequently. Remove from heat; stir in remaining 1 tablespoon butter.

Summer's Best Gazpacho

Makes 6 servings

- 3 cups tomato juice
- 2½ cups finely diced tomatoes (2 large)
- 1 cup finely diced yellow or red bell pepper (1 small)
- 1 cup finely diced unpeeled cucumber
- ½ cup chunky salsa
- 1 tablespoon olive oil
- 1 clove garlic, minced
- ½ teaspoon salt
- 1 ripe avocado, diced
- ¼ cup finely chopped fresh cilantro or basil

1. Combine tomato juice, tomatoes, bell pepper, cucumber, salsa, oil, garlic and salt in large bowl; mix well. Cover and refrigerate at least 1 hour or up to 24 hours.
2. Stir in avocado and cilantro just before serving.

Creamy Chile Corn Chowder

Makes 4 to 6 servings

- 2 tablespoons butter
- 1 cup chopped onion
- 2 Anaheim or poblano chile peppers,* seeded and diced
- ½ cup thinly sliced celery
- 1 package (16 ounces) frozen corn
- 12 ounces unpeeled new red potatoes, diced
- 4 cups whole milk
- 6 ounces cream cheese, cubed
- 2 teaspoons salt
- ¾ teaspoon black pepper

**Anaheim chiles are medium-sized green peppers with a long narrow shape and mild flavor.*

1. Melt butter in large saucepan over medium-high heat. Add onion, Anaheim peppers and celery; cook and stir 5 minutes or until onion is translucent.
2. Stir in corn, potatoes and milk; bring to a boil. Reduce heat to medium-low; cover and simmer 10 minutes or until potatoes are tender.
3. Remove from heat; add cream cheese, salt and black pepper. Stir until cream cheese is melted.

Chicken & Turkey

One-Pot Chinese Chicken Soup

Makes 4 servings

- **6 cups chicken broth**
- **2 cups water**
- **1 pound boneless skinless chicken thighs**
- **⅓ cup reduced-sodium soy sauce**
- **1 package (16 ounces) frozen stir-fry vegetables**
- **6 ounces uncooked dried thin Chinese egg noodles**
- **1 to 3 tablespoons sriracha sauce**

1. Combine broth, water, chicken and soy sauce in medium saucepan; bring to a boil over high heat. Reduce heat to low; cover and simmer 20 minutes or until chicken is cooked through and very tender. Remove chicken to plate; let stand until cool enough to handle.
2. Meanwhile, add vegetables and noodles to broth in saucepan; bring to a boil over high heat. Reduce heat to medium-high; cook 5 minutes or until noodles are tender and vegetables are heated through, stirring occasionally.
3. Shred chicken into bite-size pieces. Stir chicken and 1 tablespoon sriracha into soup; taste and add additional sriracha for a spicier flavor.

Rotisserie Chicken Noodle Soup

Make about 8 servings

- ½ (9-ounce) package no-boil lasagna noodles*
- 1 tablespoon olive oil or butter
- 2 large carrots, chopped
- 2 stalks celery, chopped
- 1 small onion, chopped
- 1 clove garlic, minced
- ½ teaspoon dried thyme
- ½ teaspoon dried oregano
- ¼ teaspoon dried basil
- 8 cups chicken broth
- 1 teaspoon salt
- ½ teaspoon black pepper
- 1 bay leaf
- 2 cups shredded rotisserie chicken
- 2 tablespoons finely chopped fresh parsley

**Or substitute 4 to 6 ounces uncooked egg noodles and omit step 1. Add uncooked noodles to soup as directed in step 5.*

1. Spread lasagna noodles in 13×9-inch baking dish or other shallow pan; cover with hot water. Let soak 10 minutes to soften, moving noodles around occasionally to prevent sticking to each other.
2. Meanwhile, heat oil in large saucepan or Dutch oven over medium heat. Add carrots, celery and onion; cook about 8 minutes or until vegetables are softened, stirring occasionally.
3. Add garlic, thyme, oregano and basil; cook and stir 2 minutes. Stir in broth, salt, pepper and bay leaf; bring to a boil over high heat.
4. Drain noodles, cut into 3×¾-inch strips. (Cut noodles crosswise into ¾-inch-wide strips, then cut each strip in half.)
5. Add noodles and chicken to broth mixture; return to a boil. Cook over medium heat 10 minutes or until noodles are tender, stirring frequently. Remove and discard bay leaf; stir in parsley.

Turkey Vegetable Rice Soup

Makes 6 servings

- 1½ pounds turkey drumsticks (2 small)
- 8 cups cold water
- 1 medium onion, cut into quarters
- 2 tablespoons soy sauce
- ¼ teaspoon black pepper
- 1 bay leaf
- 2 carrots, sliced
- ⅓ cup uncooked rice
- 4 ounces mushrooms, sliced
- 1 cup fresh snow peas, cut in half crosswise
- 1 cup coarsely chopped bok choy

1. Place drumsticks in large saucepan or Dutch oven. Add water, onion, soy sauce, pepper and bay leaf; bring to a boil over high heat. Reduce heat to medium-low; simmer, uncovered, 1½ hours or until turkey is tender.
2. Remove turkey to plate; let stand until cool enough to handle. Let broth cool slightly; skim fat. Remove and discard bay leaf. Remove turkey meat from bones; discard skin and bones. Cut turkey into bite-size pieces.
3. Add carrots and rice to broth in saucepan; bring to a boil over high heat. Reduce heat to medium-low; cook 10 minutes.
4. Add mushrooms and turkey to soup; bring to a boil over high heat. Reduce heat to medium-low; cook 5 minutes. Add snow peas and bok choy; bring to a boil over high heat. Reduce heat to medium-low; cook 8 minutes or until rice and vegetables are tender.

Chicken and Gnocchi Soup

Makes 6 to 8 servings

- ¼ cup (½ stick) butter
- 1 tablespoon extra virgin olive oil
- 1 cup finely diced onion
- 2 stalks celery, finely chopped
- 2 cloves garlic, minced
- ¼ cup all-purpose flour
- 4 cups half-and-half
- 1 can (about 14 ounces) chicken broth
- 1 teaspoon salt
- ½ teaspoon dried thyme
- ½ teaspoon dried parsley flakes
- ¼ teaspoon ground nutmeg
- 1 package (about 16 ounces) uncooked gnocchi
- 1 package (6 ounces) fully cooked chicken strips, chopped *or* 1 cup diced cooked chicken
- 1 cup shredded carrots
- 1 cup coarsely chopped fresh spinach

1. Melt butter in large saucepan or Dutch oven over medium heat; add oil. Add onion, celery and garlic; cook 8 minutes or until vegetables are softened and onion is translucent, stirring occasionally.
2. Whisk in flour; cook and stir 1 minute. Whisk in half-and-half; cook 15 minutes or until thickened, stirring occasionally.
3. Whisk in broth, salt, thyme, parsley flakes and nutmeg; cook 10 minutes or until soup is slightly thickened, stirring occasionally.
4. Add gnocchi, chicken, carrots and spinach; cook 5 minutes or until gnocchi are heated through.

Chicken Enchilada Soup

Makes 8 to 10 servings

- 2 tablespoons vegetable oil, divided
- 1½ pounds boneless skinless chicken breasts, cut into ½-inch pieces
- ½ cup chopped onion
- 2 cloves garlic, minced
- 2 cans (about 14 ounces each) chicken broth
- 3 cups water, divided
- 1 cup masa harina
- 1 package (16 ounces) pasteurized process cheese product, cubed
- 1 can (10 ounces) mild red enchilada sauce
- 1 teaspoon chili powder
- ½ teaspoon salt
- ½ teaspoon ground cumin
- 1 large tomato, seeded and chopped
- Crispy tortilla strips*

***If tortilla strips are not available, crumble tortilla chips into bite-size pieces.**

1 Heat 1 tablespoon oil in large saucepan or Dutch oven over medium-high heat. Add chicken; cook and stir 10 minutes or until no longer pink. Transfer to medium bowl with slotted spoon; drain any excess liquid from saucepan.

2 Heat remaining 1 tablespoon oil in same saucepan over medium-high heat. Add onion and garlic; cook and stir 3 minutes or until softened. Stir in broth.

3 Whisk 2 cups water into masa harina in large bowl until smooth. Whisk mixture into broth in saucepan. Stir in remaining 1 cup water, cheese product, enchilada sauce, chili powder, salt and cumin; bring to a boil over high heat. Stir in chicken. Reduce heat to medium-low; simmer, uncovered, 30 minutes, stirring frequently. Serve soup topped with tomato and tortilla strips.

Southwest Corn and Turkey Soup

Makes 6 servings

- 2 dried ancho chiles (each about 4 inches long) *or* 6 dried New Mexico chiles (about 6 inches long)
- 1 tablespoon vegetable oil
- 1 medium onion, thinly sliced
- 3 cloves garlic, minced
- 1 teaspoon ground cumin
- 3 cans (about 14 ounces each) chicken broth
- 2 small zucchini, cut into ½-inch slices
- 1½ to 2 cups shredded cooked turkey
- 1 can (about 15 ounces) black beans or chickpeas, rinsed and drained
- 1 package (10 ounces) frozen corn
- ¼ cup yellow cornmeal
- 1 teaspoon dried oregano
- ¾ teaspoon salt
- ⅓ cup chopped fresh cilantro

1. Cut stems from chiles; remove and discard seeds. Place chiles in medium bowl; cover with boiling water. Let stand 20 to 40 minutes or until softened.
2. Drain chiles; cut open lengthwise and lay flat on work surface. Scrape chile pulp from skin with edge of small knife. Finely mince pulp.
3. Heat oil in large saucepan over medium heat. Add onion; cook and stir 4 minutes. Add garlic and cumin; cook and stir 30 seconds. Stir in broth, chile pulp, zucchini, turkey, beans, corn, cornmeal, oregano and salt; bring to a boil over high heat. Reduce heat to low; simmer, uncovered, 15 minutes or until zucchini is tender. Stir in cilantro just before serving.

Skillet Chicken Soup

Makes 6 servings

- 1 teaspoon salt
- 1 teaspoon paprika
- ¼ teaspoon black pepper
- 12 ounces boneless skinless chicken breasts or thighs, cut into ¾-inch pieces
- 1 tablespoon olive oil
- 1 large onion, chopped
- 1 red bell pepper, cut into ½-inch pieces
- 3 cloves garlic, minced
- 3 cups chicken broth
- 1 can (19 ounces) cannellini beans or small white beans, rinsed and drained
- 3 cups sliced savoy or napa cabbage
- ½ cup herb-flavored croutons, slightly crushed (optional)

1. Combine salt, paprika and pepper in medium bowl; mix well. Add chicken; toss to coat.
2. Heat oil in large skillet over medium-high heat. Add chicken, onion, bell pepper and garlic; cook and stir 8 minutes or until chicken is cooked through.
3. Stir in broth and beans; bring to a simmer. Reduce heat to medium-low; cover and cook 5 minutes.
4. Stir in cabbage; cover and cook 3 minutes or until cabbage is wilted. Top with crushed croutons, if desired.

North African Chicken Soup

Makes 4 servings

- **1 teaspoon salt**
- **¾ teaspoon paprika**
- **½ teaspoon ground ginger**
- **½ teaspoon ground cumin**
- **½ teaspoon ground allspice**
- **8 ounces boneless skinless chicken breasts, cut into bite-size pieces**
- **1 tablespoon vegetable oil**
- **2½ cups chicken broth**
- **2 cups peeled sweet potato, cut into ½-inch pieces**
- **1 cup chopped onion**
- **½ cup water**
- **3 cloves garlic, minced**
- **1 teaspoon sugar**
- **2 cups canned tomatoes, undrained, coarsely chopped**
- **Black pepper**

1. Combine salt, paprika, ginger, cumin and allspice in small bowl; mix well. Combine 1½ teaspoons spice mixture and chicken in medium bowl; toss to coat.
2. Heat oil in large saucepan or Dutch oven over medium-high heat. Add chicken; cook and stir 3 to 4 minutes or until cooked through. Remove to plate.
3. Add broth, sweet potato, onion, water, garlic, sugar and remaining spice mixture to same saucepan; bring to a boil over high heat. Reduce heat to medium-low; cover and simmer 10 minutes or until sweet potato is tender.
4. Stir in tomatoes and chicken; cook until heated through. Season to taste with pepper.

Curried Turkey Noodle Soup

Makes 4 to 6 servings

- 1 tablespoon olive oil
- 12 ounces turkey tenderloin, cut into bite-size pieces
- 5 cups water
- 2 packages (3 ounces each) chicken-flavored ramen noodles
- 1 tablespoon curry powder
- ⅛ teaspoon salt
- 1 cup sliced celery
- 1 medium apple, chopped (1½ cups)
- ¼ cup dry roasted peanuts

1. Heat oil in large saucepan over medium-high heat. Add turkey; cook and stir 3 to 4 minutes or until no longer pink. Remove to plate.
2. Add water, seasoning packets from noodles, curry powder and salt to saucepan; bring to a boil. Reduce heat to low; cover and simmer 5 minutes.
3. Break up noodles. Gently stir noodles and celery into soup; bring to a boil. Reduce heat to low; simmer, uncovered, 5 minutes.
4. Stir in turkey and apple; cook 3 minutes or until heated through. Sprinkle with peanuts.

Spicy Thai Coconut Soup

Makes 4 servings

- 2 cups chicken broth
- 1 can (13½ ounces) light coconut milk
- 1 tablespoon minced fresh ginger
- ½ to 1 teaspoon red curry paste
- 3 cups coarsely shredded cooked chicken
- 1 can (15 ounces) straw mushrooms, drained
- 1 can (about 8 ounces) baby corn, drained
- 2 tablespoons lime juice
- ¼ cup chopped fresh cilantro

1. Combine broth, coconut milk, ginger and curry paste in large saucepan; mix well. Add chicken, mushrooms and baby corn; bring to a simmer over medium heat. Cook until heated through, stirring occasionally.
2. Stir in lime juice. Sprinkle with cilantro just before serving.

Note

Red curry paste can be found in jars in the Asian food section of large grocery stores. Spice levels can vary between brands—start with ½ teaspoon, then add more as desired.

Cajun-Style Chicken Soup

Makes 6 servings

- 1½ pounds bone-in skin-on chicken thighs
- 4 cups chicken broth
- 1 can (8 ounces) tomato sauce
- 1 medium onion, chopped
- 2 stalks celery, sliced
- 2 cloves garlic, minced
- 2 bay leaves
- 1 teaspoon salt
- ½ teaspoon ground cumin
- ¼ teaspoon paprika
- ¼ teaspoon ground red pepper
- ¼ teaspoon black pepper
- Dash white pepper
- 1 large green bell pepper, chopped
- ⅓ cup uncooked rice
- 8 ounces fresh or frozen okra, cut into ½-inch slices
- Hot pepper sauce (optional)

1. Combine chicken, broth, tomato sauce, onion, celery, garlic, bay leaves, salt, cumin, paprika, red pepper, black pepper and white pepper in large saucepan or Dutch oven; bring to a boil over high heat. Reduce heat to medium-low; simmer, uncovered, 1 hour or until chicken is tender, skimming foam that rises to the surface.
2. Remove chicken to plate; let stand until cool enough to handle. Skim fat from soup. Remove chicken meat from bones; discard skin and bones. Cut chicken into bite-size pieces.
3. Add chicken, bell pepper and rice to soup; bring to a boil over high heat. Reduce heat to medium-low; cook, uncovered, about 12 minutes or until rice is tender.
4. Add okra; cook 8 minutes or until okra is tender. Remove and discard bay leaves. Serve soup with hot pepper sauce, if desired.

Cock-A-Leekie Soup

Makes 6 to 8 servings

- 4 cups reduced-sodium chicken broth
- 4 cups water
- 2½ pounds chicken thighs (with bones and skin)
- 3 stalks celery, sliced
- 2 bay leaves
- 5 to 6 large leeks (about 2½ pounds)
- ½ cup uncooked pearl barley
- 1 teaspoon salt
- 1 teaspoon ground allspice
- 12 pitted prunes, halved
- Black pepper

1 Combine broth, water, chicken, celery and bay leaves in large saucepan or Dutch oven; bring to a boil over high heat. Reduce heat to low; cover and simmer 30 minutes or until chicken is tender. Remove chicken to plate; let stand until cool enough to handle.

2 Meanwhile, trim leeks. Cut off roots, any damaged leaves and very tough tops. Cut in half lengthwise, then cut crosswise into ¾-inch pieces. Wash well in several changes of water.

3 Add leeks, barley, salt and allspice to broth in saucepan; cover and simmer 40 minutes or until leeks and barley are tender.

4 Remove chicken meat from bones; discard skin and bones. Cut chicken into bite-size pieces. Add chicken to soup with prunes; cook 3 minutes or until prunes soften. Remove and discard bay leaves. Season with additional salt and pepper.

Rustic Country Turkey Soup

Makes 4 servings

- 2 tablespoons olive oil
- 1 cup chopped onion
- ¾ cup sliced carrots
- 4 ounces sliced mushrooms
- 1 teaspoon minced garlic
- 2 cans (about 14 ounces each) chicken broth
- 2 ounces uncooked multigrain rotini pasta
- 1 teaspoon dried thyme
- ½ teaspoon poultry seasoning
- ¼ teaspoon salt
- ⅛ teaspoon red pepper flakes
- 2 cups chopped cooked turkey
- ¼ cup chopped fresh parsley

1. Heat oil in large saucepan over medium-high heat. Add onion and carrots; cook and stir 2 minutes. Add mushrooms; cook 2 minutes. Add garlic; cook and stir 30 seconds. Stir in broth; bring to a boil.
2. Stir in pasta, thyme, poultry seasoning, salt and red pepper flakes; return to a boil. Reduce heat to low; cover and cook 8 minutes or until pasta is tender.
3. Stir in turkey and parsley; cook 2 to 3 minutes or until heated through.

Coconut Curry Chicken Soup

Makes 4 servings

- 3 cups chicken broth
- 8 boneless skinless chicken thighs
- 1 cup chopped onion, divided
- 1 teaspoon salt, divided
- 4 whole cloves
- 1 tablespoon butter
- 2 tablespoons curry powder
- 1¼ cups coconut milk
- ¼ cup plus 1 tablespoon chopped fresh mint, divided
- 3 tablespoons chopped crystallized ginger
- ¼ teaspoon ground cloves
- 1 cup half-and-half
- 2 cups cooked rice (optional)
- Lime wedges (optional)

1. Bring broth to a boil in large skillet over high heat. Add chicken, ½ cup onion, ½ teaspoon salt and whole cloves; return to a boil. Reduce heat to low; cover and simmer 40 minutes or until chicken is very tender.

2. Remove chicken to plate; set aside until cool enough to handle. Pour cooking liquid from skillet into large glass measuring cup or bowl; discard onion and cloves.

3. Melt butter in same skillet over medium-high heat. Add remaining ½ cup onion; cook and stir 4 minutes or until onion is translucent. Add curry powder; cook and stir 20 seconds or just until fragrant. Reduce heat to medium-low. Return cooking liquid to skillet with coconut milk, 1 tablespoon mint, ginger, ground cloves and remaining ½ teaspoon salt; cover and simmer 10 minutes.

4. Shred chicken into bite-size pieces. Add to soup with half-and-half; cook 3 minutes or until heated through. Sprinkle with remaining ¼ cup mint. Serve with rice and lime wedges, if desired.

Spicy Squash and Chicken Soup

Makes 4 servings

- 1 tablespoon vegetable oil
- 1 small onion, finely chopped
- 1 stalk celery, finely chopped
- 2 cups chicken broth
- 2 cups cubed butternut or delicata squash (about 1 small)
- 1 can (about 14 ounces) diced tomatoes with green chiles
- 1 cup chopped cooked chicken
- 1 teaspoon salt
- ½ teaspoon ground ginger
- ⅛ teaspoon ground cumin
- ⅛ teaspoon black pepper
- 2 teaspoons lime juice
- Fresh parsley or cilantro sprigs (optional)

1. Heat oil in large saucepan over medium heat. Add onion and celery; cook and stir 5 minutes or until vegetables are tender.
2. Stir in broth, squash, tomatoes, chicken, salt, ginger, cumin and pepper; bring to a boil. Reduce heat to low; cover and simmer 30 minutes or until squash is tender. Stir in lime juice. Garnish with parsley.

Pozole

Makes 4 to 6 servings

- 1 tablespoon olive oil
- 1 large onion, thinly sliced
- 2 teaspoons dried oregano
- 1 clove garlic, minced
- ½ teaspoon ground cumin
- 2 cans (about 14 ounces each) chicken broth
- 1 package (10 ounces) frozen corn
- 2 cans (4 ounces each) diced green chiles
- 1 can (2¼ ounces) sliced black olives, drained
- ½ teaspoon salt
- 12 ounces boneless skinless chicken breasts
- Chopped fresh cilantro (optional)

1. Heat oil in large saucepan over low heat. Add onion, oregano, garlic and cumin; cover and cook about 6 minutes or until onion is tender, stirring occasionally.
2. Stir in broth, corn, chiles, olives and salt; bring to a boil over high heat.
3. Meanwhile, cut chicken into thin strips. Add to saucepan; cover and cook over medium-low heat 4 minutes or until chicken is cooked through. Garnish with cilantro.

Tortilla Soup

Makes 4 servings

Vegetable oil

3 (6- or 7-inch) corn tortillas, halved and cut into strips

½ cup chopped onion

1 clove garlic, minced

2 cans (about 14 ounces each) chicken broth

1 can (about 14 ounces) diced tomatoes

1 cup shredded cooked chicken

2 teaspoons lime juice

1 small avocado, diced

2 tablespoons chopped fresh cilantro

1 Pour oil into small skillet to depth of ½ inch; heat over medium-high heat to 360°F. Add tortilla strips, a few at a time; cook 1 minute or until crisp and lightly browned. Remove to paper towel-lined plate with slotted spoon.*

2 Heat 2 teaspoons oil in large saucepan over medium heat. Add onion and garlic; cook 6 to 8 minutes or until onion is softened, stirring occasionally. Stir in broth and tomatoes; bring to a boil. Reduce heat to low; cover and simmer 15 minutes.

3 Stir in chicken and lime juice; cook 5 minutes. Top soup with tortilla strips, avocado and cilantro.

**To save time, you can purchase fried or baked tortilla strips at the supermarket. Proceed with recipe as directed, beginning with step 2.*

Beef & Pork

Beefy Broccoli and Cheese Soup

Makes 4 servings

- **4 ounces ground beef**
- **2 cups beef broth**
- **1 bag (10 ounces) frozen chopped broccoli, thawed**
- **¼ cup chopped onion**
- **1 cup milk**
- **2 tablespoons all-purpose flour**
- **1 cup (4 ounces) shredded sharp Cheddar cheese**
- **1½ teaspoons chopped fresh oregano *or* ½ teaspoon dried oregano**
- **Salt and black pepper**
- **Hot pepper sauce**

1. Cook beef in large skillet over medium-high heat 6 to 8 minutes or until browned, stirring to break up meat. Drain fat.
2. Pour broth into medium saucepan; bring to a boil over medium-high heat. Add broccoli and onion; cook 5 minutes or until broccoli is tender. Stir milk into flour in small bowl until smooth.
3. Stir milk mixture and ground beef into saucepan; cook and stir until soup is thickened and heated through.
4. Add cheese and oregano; stir until cheese is melted. Season with salt, black pepper and hot pepper sauce.

Corned Beef and Cabbage Soup

Makes about 8 servings

- 1 tablespoon vegetable oil
- 1 onion, chopped
- 2 stalks celery, chopped
- 2 carrots, chopped
- 2 cloves garlic, minced
- 4 to 5 cups coarsely chopped green cabbage (about half of small head)
- 12 ounces unpeeled Yukon gold potatoes, chopped
- 4 cups beef broth
- 4 cups water
- ½ cup quick-cooking barley
- 1 teaspoon salt
- 1 teaspoon dried thyme
- ½ teaspoon black pepper
- ¼ teaspoon ground mustard
- 12 ounces corned beef (leftovers or deli corned beef, about 2½ cups), cut into ½-inch pieces

1. Heat oil in large saucepan or Dutch oven over medium-high heat. Add onion, celery and carrots; cook 5 minutes or until vegetables are softened, stirring occasionally. Add garlic; cook and stir 1 minute.
2. Stir in cabbage, potatoes, broth, water, barley, salt, thyme, pepper and mustard; bring to a boil. Reduce heat to medium-low; simmer, uncovered, 20 minutes, stirring occasionally.
3. Stir in corned beef; cook 10 to 15 minutes or until potatoes are tender. Season with additional salt and pepper.

Sausage Rice Soup

Makes 4 to 6 servings

- 2 teaspoons olive oil
- 8 ounces Italian sausage, casings removed
- 1 small onion, chopped
- ½ teaspoon fennel seeds
- 1 tablespoon tomato paste
- 4 cups chicken broth
- 1 can (about 14 ounces) whole tomatoes, undrained, crushed with hands or coarsely chopped
- 1½ cups water
- ½ cup uncooked rice
- ¼ teaspoon salt
- ⅛ teaspoon black pepper
- 2 to 3 ounces baby spinach
- ⅓ cup shredded mozzarella cheese (optional)

1. Heat oil in large saucepan or Dutch oven over medium-high heat. Add sausage; cook 8 minutes or until browned, stirring to break up meat. Add onion; cook and stir 5 minutes or until softened. Add fennel seeds; cook and stir 30 seconds. Add tomato paste; cook and stir 1 minute.
2. Stir in broth, tomatoes with juice, water, rice, salt and pepper; bring to a boil. Reduce heat to medium-low; cook, uncovered, 18 minutes or until rice is tender.
3. Stir in spinach; cook 3 minutes or until wilted. Season with additional salt and pepper. Sprinkle with cheese, if desired, just before serving.

Beef Vegetable Soup

Makes 6 to 8 servings

- **1½ pounds cubed beef stew meat**
- **¼ cup all-purpose flour**
- **3 tablespoons vegetable oil, divided**
- **1 onion, chopped**
- **2 stalks celery, chopped**
- **3 tablespoons tomato paste**
- **2 teaspoons salt**
- **1 teaspoon dried thyme**
- **½ teaspoon garlic powder**
- **¼ teaspoon black pepper**
- **6 cups beef broth, divided**
- **1 can (28 ounces) stewed tomatoes, undrained**
- **1 tablespoon Worcestershire sauce**
- **1 bay leaf**
- **4 unpeeled red potatoes (about 1 pound), cut into 1-inch pieces**
- **3 medium carrots, cut in half lengthwise and cut into ½-inch slices**
- **6 ounces green beans, trimmed and cut into 1-inch pieces**
- **1 cup frozen corn**

1. Combine beef and flour in medium bowl; toss to coat. Heat 1 tablespoon oil in large saucepan or Dutch oven over medium-high heat. Cook beef in two batches about 5 minutes or until browned, adding additional 1 tablespoon oil after first batch. Remove beef to medium bowl.
2. Heat remaining 1 tablespoon oil in same saucepan. Add onion and celery; cook and stir 5 minutes or until vegetables are softened. Add tomato paste, salt, thyme, garlic powder and pepper; cook and stir 1 minute. Stir in 1 cup broth, scraping up browned bits from bottom of saucepan. Stir in remaining 5 cups broth, tomatoes with juice, Worcestershire sauce, bay leaf and beef; bring to a boil.
3. Reduce heat to low; cover and simmer 1 hour and 20 minutes. Add potatoes and carrots; cook 15 minutes.
4. Add green beans and corn; cook 15 minutes or until vegetables are tender. Remove and discard bay leaf before serving.

Hot and Sour Soup

Makes 4 servings

- 1 package (1 ounce) dried shiitake mushrooms
- 4 ounces firm tofu, drained
- 4 cups chicken broth
- 3 tablespoons white vinegar
- 2 tablespoons soy sauce
- ½ to 1 teaspoon hot chili oil
- ¼ teaspoon white pepper
- 1 cup shredded cooked pork
- ½ cup drained canned bamboo shoots, cut into thin strips
- 3 tablespoons water
- 2 tablespoons cornstarch
- 1 egg white, lightly beaten
- ¼ cup thinly sliced green onions or chopped fresh cilantro
- 1 teaspoon dark sesame oil

1. Place mushrooms in small bowl; cover with warm water. Soak 20 minutes to soften. Drain mushrooms; squeeze out excess water. Discard stems; slice caps.
2. Press tofu lightly between paper towels; cut into ½-inch squares or triangles.
3. Combine broth, vinegar, soy sauce, chili oil and white pepper in medium saucepan; bring to a boil over high heat. Reduce heat to medium-low; cook 2 minutes.
4. Stir in mushrooms, tofu, pork and bamboo shoots; cook and stir until heated through.
5. Stir water into cornstarch in small bowl until smooth. Stir into soup until blended; cook 4 minutes or until soup boils and thickens, stirring frequently. Remove from heat.
6. Stirring constantly in one direction, slowly pour egg white into soup in thin, steady stream. Stir in green onions and sesame oil. Serve immediately.

Beef Barley Soup

Makes 4 servings

- 1 tablespoon olive oil
- 12 ounces boneless beef top round steak, cut into ½-inch pieces
- 3 cans (about 14 ounces each) beef broth
- 2 cups unpeeled cubed potatoes
- 1 can (about 14 ounces) diced tomatoes
- 1 cup chopped onion
- 1 cup sliced carrots
- ½ cup uncooked pearl barley
- 1 tablespoon cider vinegar
- 2 teaspoons caraway seeds
- 2 teaspoons dried marjoram
- 2 teaspoons dried thyme
- 1 teaspoon salt
- ½ teaspoon black pepper
- 1½ cups sliced green beans (½-inch slices)

1. Heat oil in large saucepan or Dutch oven over medium-high heat. Add beef; cook about 5 minutes or until browned on all sides, stirring occasionally.
2. Stir in broth, potatoes, tomatoes, onion, carrots, barley, vinegar, caraway seeds, marjoram, thyme, salt and pepper; bring to a boil over high heat. Reduce heat to low; cover and simmer 1½ hours.
3. Stir in green beans; simmer, uncovered, 30 minutes or until beef is fork-tender.

Hearty Tuscan Soup

Makes 6 to 8 servings

- 1 teaspoon olive oil
- 1 pound bulk mild or hot Italian sausage*
- 1 medium onion, chopped
- 3 cloves garlic, minced
- ¼ cup all-purpose flour
- 5 cups chicken broth
- 1 teaspoon salt
- ½ teaspoon Italian seasoning
- 3 medium unpeeled russet potatoes (about 1 pound), halved lengthwise and thinly sliced
- 2 cups packed torn stemmed kale leaves
- 1 cup half-and-half or whipping cream

**Or use sausage links and remove from casings.*

1 Heat oil in large saucepan or Dutch oven over medium-high heat. Add sausage; cook until sausage begins to brown, stirring to break up meat. Add onion and garlic; cook about 5 minutes or until onion is softened and sausage is browned, stirring occasionally.

2 Stir in flour until blended. Add broth, salt and Italian seasoning; bring to a boil. Stir in potatoes and kale. Reduce heat to medium-low; cook 15 to 20 minutes or until potatoes are fork-tender.

3 Reduce heat to low; stir in half-and-half. Cook about 5 minutes or until heated through.

Vietnamese Beef Soup (Pho)

Makes 6 servings

- **12 ounces boneless beef top sirloin or top round steak**
- **4 ounces thin rice noodles (rice sticks)**
- **6 cups beef broth**
- **3 cups water**
- **2 tablespoons minced fresh ginger**
- **2 tablespoons reduced-sodium soy sauce**
- **1 cinnamon stick (3 inches long)**
- **½ cup thinly sliced carrots**
- **2 cups fresh bean sprouts**
- **1 red onion, halved and thinly sliced**
- **½ cup chopped fresh cilantro**
- **½ cup chopped fresh basil**
- **2 minced jalapeño peppers *or* 1 to 3 teaspoons chili sauce**

1. Freeze beef 45 minutes or just until firm. Place rice noodles in large bowl; cover with hot water and soak 20 minutes or until soft. Drain noodles.
2. Meanwhile, combine broth, water, ginger, soy sauce and cinnamon stick in large saucepan; bring to a boil over high heat. Reduce heat to low; cover and simmer 20 minutes. Remove and discard cinnamon stick.
3. Slice beef lengthwise in half, then slice crosswise into very thin strips. Add noodles and carrots to simmering broth; cook 3 minutes or until carrots are tender. Add beef and bean sprouts; cook 1 minute or until beef is no longer pink.
4. Remove from heat; stir in onion, cilantro, basil and jalapeños.

Tip

Rice noodles are semi-translucent dried noodles that come in many sizes and have many names, including rice stick noodles, rice-flour noodles and pho noodles. Widths range from very thin (called rice vermicelli) to 1 inch wide.

Italian-Style Meatball Soup

Makes 8 servings

- 8 ounces ground beef
- 4 ounces bulk Italian sausage
- 1 onion, finely chopped, divided
- ⅓ cup plain dry bread crumbs
- 1 egg
- ½ teaspoon salt
- 4 cups vegetable or beef broth
- 2 cups water
- 1 can (about 14 ounces) stewed tomatoes
- 1 can (8 ounces) pizza sauce
- 2 cups sliced cabbage
- 1 can (about 15 ounces) kidney beans, rinsed and drained
- 2 carrots, sliced
- ½ cup frozen Italian green beans

1. Combine beef, sausage, 2 tablespoons chopped onion, bread crumbs, egg and salt in large bowl; mix well. Shape into 32 (1-inch) meatballs.
2. Brown half of meatballs in large skillet over medium heat, turning frequently. Remove to paper towel-lined plate. Repeat with remaining meatballs.
3. Combine broth, water, tomatoes and pizza sauce in large saucepan or Dutch oven; bring to a boil over medium-high heat. Add meatballs, remaining onion, cabbage, kidney beans and carrots; bring to a boil. Reduce heat to medium-low; simmer, uncovered, 20 minutes.
4. Stir in green beans; cook 10 minutes.

Pork and Cabbage Soup

Makes 6 servings

- 8 ounces pork loin, cut into ½-inch pieces
- 1 medium onion, chopped
- 2 slices bacon, finely chopped
- 1 can (about 28 ounces) whole tomatoes, drained and coarsely chopped
- 2 cups reduced-sodium chicken broth
- 2 cups reduced-sodium beef broth
- 2 medium carrots, sliced
- 1 teaspoon salt
- 1 bay leaf
- ¾ teaspoon dried marjoram
- ⅛ teaspoon black pepper
- ½ medium cabbage, chopped
- 2 tablespoons chopped fresh parsley

1. Combine pork, onion and bacon in large saucepan or Dutch oven; cook over medium heat about 5 minutes until pork is no longer pink and onion is tender, stirring frequently.
2. Stir in tomatoes, chicken broth, beef broth, carrots, salt, bay leaf, marjoram and pepper; bring to a boil over high heat. Reduce heat to medium-low; simmer, uncovered, about 30 minutes. Remove and discard bay leaf. Skim off fat.
3. Add cabbage; bring to a boil over high heat. Reduce heat to medium-low; cook, uncovered, about 15 minutes or until cabbage is tender. Stir in parsley.

Beef Goulash Soup

Makes 6 to 8 servings

- 1 tablespoon vegetable oil
- 1¼ pounds boneless beef sirloin tri-tip roast,* cut into 1-inch pieces
- 1 cup chopped onion
- 3 cans (about 14 ounces each) beef broth
- 2 cans (about 14 ounces each) diced tomatoes
- 1½ cups sliced carrots
- 2 tablespoons sugar
- 1 tablespoon paprika
- 1 tablespoon caraway seeds, slightly crushed
- 2 cloves garlic, minced
- 1 teaspoon salt
- 4 ounces (about 2 cups) uncooked egg or whole wheat noodles
- 2 cups thinly sliced cabbage or coleslaw mix

**Or substitute chuck roast or beef round steak.*

1. Heat oil in large saucepan or Dutch oven over medium heat. Cook beef in two batches until browned; remove to plate. Drain fat.
2. Add onion to saucepan; cook 3 minutes or until tender, scraping up browned bits from bottom of saucepan.
3. Return beef to saucepan. Stir in broth, tomatoes, carrots, sugar, paprika, caraway seeds, garlic and salt; bring to a boil. Reduce heat to medium-low; cover and simmer 45 minutes or until beef is tender.
4. Stir in noodles; bring to a boil. Reduce heat to medium-low; cook 10 minutes or until noodles are tender. Stir in cabbage; cook 2 minutes or until heated through.

Sausage and Lentil Soup

Makes 4 to 6 servings

- 8 ounces bulk hot Italian sausage
- 1 onion, chopped
- 2 cloves garlic, minced
- 1 stalk celery, chopped
- 1 carrot, chopped
- 1 small zucchini, chopped
- 3 to 3½ cups chicken broth, divided
- 1 can (about 14 ounces) diced tomatoes
- 1 cup dried lentils, rinsed and sorted
- ½ teaspoon salt
- ½ teaspoon dried oregano
- ½ teaspoon dried basil
- ¼ teaspoon dried thyme
- ¼ teaspoon black pepper
- Chopped fresh basil and grated Parmesan cheese (optional)

1. Cook sausage in large saucepan or Dutch oven over medium-high heat 8 minutes or until browned, stirring to break up meat.
2. Add onion; cook and stir 3 minutes or until onion begins to soften. Add garlic; cook and stir 1 minute. Add celery, carrot and zucchini; cook 3 minutes, stirring occasionally.
3. Stir in 3 cups broth, tomatoes, lentils, salt, oregano, dried basil, thyme and pepper; bring to a boil. Reduce heat to low; cover and simmer about 1 hour or until lentils are tender. Add additional broth, if necessary, to thin soup. Garnish with fresh basil and cheese.

Sweet Potato and Ham Soup

Makes 6 servings

- 1 tablespoon butter
- 1 leek, thinly sliced
- 1 clove garlic, minced
- 4 cups chicken broth
- 2 sweet potatoes, peeled and cut into ¾-inch pieces
- 8 ounces ham, cut into ½-inch pieces
- ½ teaspoon dried thyme
- 2 ounces stemmed fresh spinach, coarsely chopped

1. Melt butter in large saucepan over medium heat. Add leek and garlic; cook and stir about 3 minutes or until tender.
2. Stir in broth, sweet potatoes, ham and thyme; bring to a boil over high heat. Reduce heat to low; simmer, uncovered, 10 minutes or until sweet potatoes are tender.
3. Stir in spinach; cook 2 minutes or until wilted. Serve immediately.

Beef and Beet Borscht

Makes 4 servings

- 2 cans (15 ounces each) julienned beets
- 1 cup buttermilk
- ¼ teaspoon salt
- ⅛ teaspoon black pepper
- ⅛ teaspoon ground cloves
- 1 cup beef broth
- 4 ounces thinly sliced deli roast beef, cut into strips
- ¼ cup sour cream
- Chopped fresh parsley

1. Drain beets, reserving 1 cup liquid. Place half of beets in food processor; process until finely chopped. Add buttermilk, salt, pepper and cloves; process until smooth. Transfer to medium bowl.
2. Stir in remaining beets, broth, reserved beet liquid and roast beef; mix well. Cover and refrigerate at least 2 hours or up to 24 hours.
3. Top soup with sour cream; sprinkle with parsley.

Quick and Easy Ravioli Soup

Makes 8 servings

- 8 ounces mild Italian sausage, casings removed
- ½ cup chopped onion
- 1 clove garlic, crushed
- 2 cans (about 14 ounces each) chicken broth
- 2 cups water
- 1 package (9 ounces) frozen mini cheese-filled ravioli
- 1 can (about 15 ounces) chickpeas, rinsed and drained
- 1 can (about 14 ounces) diced tomatoes with mild green chiles
- ¾ teaspoon dried oregano
- ½ teaspoon black pepper
- ¼ teaspoon salt
- 1 cup baby spinach
- Grated Parmesan cheese

1. Cook sausage, onion and garlic in large saucepan or Dutch oven over medium heat 5 minutes or until sausage is cooked through, stirring to break up meat. Drain fat. Remove to medium bowl.
2. Add broth and water to saucepan; bring to a boil over medium-high heat. Add ravioli; cook 4 to 5 minutes or until tender.
3. Return sausage mixture to saucepan with chickpeas, tomatoes, oregano, pepper and salt; cook about 5 minutes or until heated through.
4. Stir in spinach; cook 1 minute or until wilted. Sprinkle with cheese.

Seafood

Seafood Bisque

Makes 6 servings

- 2 tablespoons olive oil
- 1 onion, finely chopped
- 2 cups chicken broth
- 1 package (9 ounces) frozen artichoke hearts, thawed
- ½ cup dry white wine
- 1 pound mixed shellfish (raw shrimp, peeled and deveined; raw scallops; and/or canned crabmeat)
- 1 cup whipping cream
- 2 tablespoons chopped fresh parsley
- 1 teaspoon salt
- ½ teaspoon ground nutmeg
- ¼ teaspoon white pepper

1. Heat oil in large saucepan over medium-high heat. Add onion; cook and stir 3 minutes or until softened. Add broth, artichokes and wine; bring to a boil over medium-high heat. Reduce heat to low; cover and simmer 6 minutes.
2. Working in batches, blend soup in blender or food processor until smooth. (Or use hand-held immersion blender.). Return soup to saucepan.
3. Stir in shellfish, cream, parsley, salt, nutmeg and pepper; bring to a simmer over medium heat. Reduce heat to low; cook, uncovered, 5 minutes. (Do not boil or shellfish will become tough.)

New England Fish Chowder

Makes 4 to 6 servings

- 4 ounces bacon, chopped
- 1 cup chopped onion
- ½ cup chopped celery
- 2 cups diced peeled russet potatoes
- 2 tablespoons all-purpose flour
- 2 cups water
- 1 teaspoon salt
- 1 bay leaf
- 1 teaspoon dried dill weed
- ½ teaspoon dried thyme
- ½ teaspoon black pepper
- 1 pound cod, haddock or halibut fillets, skinned, boned and cut into 1-inch pieces
- 2 cups milk or half-and-half

1. Cook bacon in large saucepan over medium-high heat until crisp, stirring occasionally. Drain on paper towel-lined plate.
2. Add onion and celery to drippings in saucepan; cook and stir about 5 minutes or until onion is soft. Add potatoes; cook and stir 1 minute. Add flour; cook and stir 1 minute. Stir in water, salt, bay leaf, dill weed, thyme and pepper; bring to a boil over high heat. Reduce heat to low; cover and simmer 25 minutes or until potatoes are fork-tender.
3. Stir in fish; cover and simmer 5 minutes or until fish begins to flake when tested with fork. Remove and discard bay leaf.
4. Stir in bacon and milk; cook just until heated through. *Do not boil.*

Cioppino

Makes 4 servings

- 1 tablespoon olive oil
- 1 large onion, chopped
- 1 cup sliced celery
- 1 clove garlic, minced
- 4 cups water
- 1 tablespoon Italian seasoning
- 1 cube fish-flavored bouillon
- 4 ounces cod or other boneless mild-flavored fish fillets, cut into ½-inch pieces
- 1 large tomato, chopped
- 1 can (10 ounces) baby clams, rinsed and drained (optional)
- 4 ounces small raw shrimp, peeled and deveined
- 4 ounces raw bay scallops
- ¼ cup flaked crabmeat or crabmeat blend
- 2 tablespoons lemon juice

1. Heat oil in large saucepan over medium heat. Add onion, celery and garlic; cook and stir 5 minutes or until onion is soft.
2. Stir in water, Italian seasoning and bouillon; bring to a boil over high heat. Stir in fish and tomato. Reduce heat to medium-low; cook about 5 minutes or until fish is opaque.
3. Add clams, if desired, shrimp, scallops, crabmeat and lemon juice; cook about 5 minutes or just until shrimp and scallops are opaque.

Spicy Thai Shrimp Soup

Makes 4 servings

- **1 tablespoon vegetable oil**
- **1 pound medium raw shrimp, peeled and deveined, shells reserved**
- **1 jalapeño pepper, cut into slivers**
- **1 tablespoon paprika**
- **¼ teaspoon ground red pepper**
- **4 cans (about 14 ounces each) chicken broth**
- **1 (½-inch) strip *each* lemon and lime peel**
- **1 can (15 ounces) straw mushrooms, drained**
- **Juice of 1 lemon**
- **Juice of 1 lime**
- **2 tablespoons soy sauce**
- **1 red Thai pepper or red jalapeño pepper *or* ¼ small red bell pepper, cut into strips**
- **¼ cup fresh cilantro leaves**

1. Heat large saucepan over medium-high heat 1 minute. Add oil; heat 30 seconds. Add shrimp and jalapeño; cook and stir 1 minute. Add paprika and ground red pepper; cook and stir 1 minute or until shrimp are pink and opaque. Remove shrimp mixture to medium bowl.
2. Add shrimp shells to saucepan; cook and stir 30 seconds. Stir in broth and lemon and lime peels; bring to a boil. Reduce heat to low; cover and simmer 15 minutes.
3. Remove and discard shrimp shells and peels with slotted spoon. Add mushrooms and shrimp mixture to broth; bring to a boil over medium heat. Stir in lemon and lime juices, soy sauce and Thai pepper; cook just until heated through. Sprinkle with cilantro; serve immediately.

Manhattan Clam Chowder

Makes 6 servings

- **3 slices bacon, chopped**
- **1 onion, chopped**
- **2 stalks celery, diced**
- **1 carrot, diced**
- **1 clove garlic, minced**
- **1 teaspoon dried rosemary**
- **½ teaspoon dried thyme**
- **2 cans (about 14 ounces each) diced tomatoes**
- **1 can (8 ounces) tomato sauce**
- **1 bottle (8 ounces) clam juice**
- **¼ teaspoon black pepper**
- **1 bay leaf**
- **2 cans (6½ ounces each) chopped clams, undrained**

1. Cook bacon in large saucepan over medium-high heat 5 minutes, stirring frequently. Add onion, celery and carrot; cook and stir 5 minutes or until vegetables are softened.
2. Add garlic, rosemary and thyme; cook and stir 1 minute. Stir in tomatoes, tomato sauce, clam juice, pepper ad bay leaf; bring to a boil. Reduce heat to medium-low; simmer, uncovered, 15 minutes.
3. Stir in clams; cook 4 minutes or until heated through. Remove and discard bay leaf.

Savory Seafood Soup

Makes 4 servings

- 2½ cups water or chicken broth
- 1½ cups dry white wine
- 1 onion, chopped
- ½ red bell pepper, chopped
- ½ green bell pepper, chopped
- 1 clove garlic, minced
- ¼ teaspoon salt
- 8 ounces halibut, cut into 1-inch pieces
- 8 ounces sea scallops, cut into halves
- 1 teaspoon dried thyme
- Juice of ½ lime
- Dash hot pepper sauce
- Black pepper

1. Combine water, wine, onion, bell peppers, garlic and salt in large saucepan; bring to a boil over high heat. Reduce heat to medium-low; cover and simmer 15 minutes or until bell peppers are tender, stirring occasionally.
2. Add fish, scallops and thyme; cook 2 minutes or until fish and scallops are opaque. Stir in lime juice and hot pepper sauce. Season with additional salt and black pepper.

Tip

If halibut is not available, cod, ocean perch or haddock can be substituted.

Cod Chowder

Makes 6 to 8 servings

- 2 tablespoons vegetable oil
- 1 pound unpeeled red potatoes, diced
- 2 medium leeks, halved and thinly sliced
- 2 stalks celery, diced
- 1 bulb fennel, diced
- ½ yellow or red bell pepper, diced
- 2 teaspoons chopped fresh thyme
- ¾ teaspoon salt
- ½ teaspoon black pepper
- 2 tablespoons all-purpose flour
- 2 cups clam juice
- 1 cup water
- 1 cup half-and-half
- 1½ pounds cod, cut into 1-inch pieces
- 1 cup frozen corn
- ¼ cup finely chopped fresh Italian parsley

1. Heat oil in large saucepan or Dutch oven over medium heat. Add potatoes, leeks, celery, fennel, bell pepper, thyme, salt and black pepper; cover and cook about 8 minutes or until vegetables are slightly softened, stirring occasionally. Add flour; cook and stir 1 minute.
2. Stir in clam juice and water; bring to a boil over high heat. Reduce heat to medium-low; cover and simmer about 10 minutes or until potatoes are tender. Remove from heat.
3. Transfer 1½ cups soup to blender or food processor; add half-and-half and blend until smooth.
4. Add fish, corn and parsley to saucepan; bring to a simmer over medium-high heat. Stir in blended soup mixture; cover and cook over medium heat about 3 minutes or until fish is firm and opaque, stirring occasionally. Serve immediately.

Spicy Shrimp Gumbo

Makes 8 servings

- ½ cup vegetable oil
- ½ cup all-purpose flour
- 1 large onion, chopped
- ½ cup chopped fresh parsley
- ½ cup chopped celery
- ½ cup sliced green onions
- 6 cloves garlic, minced
- 4 cups chicken broth or water*
- 1 package (10 ounces) frozen sliced okra, thawed (optional)
- 1 teaspoon salt
- ½ teaspoon ground red pepper
- 2 pounds medium raw shrimp, peeled and deveined
- 3 cups hot cooked rice
- Fresh parsley sprigs (optional)

**Traditional gumbo is thick like stew. For thinner gumbo, add 1 to 2 cups additional broth.*

1. For roux, blend oil and flour in large saucepan or Dutch oven until smooth. Cook over medium heat 10 to 15 minutes or until roux is dark brown but not burned, stirring frequently.
2. Add chopped onion, chopped parsley, celery, green onions and garlic to roux; cook 5 to 10 minutes or until vegetables are tender, stirring frequently. Add broth, okra, if desired, salt and red pepper; cover and cook 15 minutes.
3. Add shrimp; cook 3 to 5 minutes or until shrimp are pink and opaque.
4. Spoon about ⅓ cup rice into each of eight shallow bowls; top with gumbo. Garnish with parsley sprigs.

Creamy Crab Chowder

Makes 6 to 8 servings

- **1 tablespoon butter**
- **1 cup finely chopped onion**
- **2 cloves garlic, minced**
- **1 cup finely chopped celery**
- **½ cup finely chopped green bell pepper**
- **½ cup finely chopped red bell pepper**
- **3 cans (about 14 ounces each) chicken broth**
- **3 cups diced peeled potatoes**
- **½ teaspoon salt**
- **1 package (10 ounces) frozen corn**
- **2 cans (6½ ounces each) lump crabmeat**
- **½ cup half-and-half**
- **¼ teaspoon black pepper**

1. Melt butter in large saucepan or Dutch oven over medium heat. Add onion and garlic; cook and stir 6 minutes or until softened but not browned. Add celery and bell peppers; cook 8 minutes or until celery is tender, stirring frequently.
2. Stir in broth, potatoes and salt; bring to a boil over high heat. Reduce heat to low; cook 10 minutes. Add corn; cook 5 minutes or until potatoes are tender.
3. Drain crabmeat; place in small bowl. Flake to break up large pieces; add to soup. Stir in half-and-half and black pepper; bring to a simmer. *Do not boil.*

Italian Fish Soup

Makes 2 servings

- 1 cup meatless pasta sauce
- ¾ cup water
- ¾ cup chicken broth
- 1 teaspoon Italian seasoning
- ½ teaspoon salt
- ¾ cup uncooked small pasta shells
- 4 ounces fresh halibut or haddock steak, 1 inch thick, skinned and cut into 1-inch pieces
- 1½ cups frozen vegetable blend, such as broccoli, carrots and water chestnuts or broccoli, carrots and cauliflower

1 Combine pasta sauce, water, broth, Italian seasoning and salt in medium saucepan; bring to a boil over high heat. Stir in pasta; return to a boil. Reduce heat to medium-low; cover and simmer 5 minutes.

2 Stir in fish and frozen vegetables; return to a boil. Reduce heat to medium-low; cover and cook 4 to 5 minutes or until pasta is tender and fish begins to flake when tested with fork.

Shrimp Gazpacho

Makes 2 servings

- 1 tablespoon olive oil
- 8 ounces medium shrimp, peeled and deveined
- ¼ teaspoon salt
- ⅛ teaspoon black pepper
- 3 plum tomatoes, chopped (about 1½ cups)
- ¼ small red onion, chopped
- ¼ cucumber, peeled and chopped
- ¼ cup finely chopped jarred roasted red peppers, divided
- 1 clove garlic, chopped
- ¾ cup tomato juice
- 1 tablespoon red wine vinegar
- Diced red and/or yellow bell pepper (optional)
- Fresh basil sprigs (optional)

1. Heat oil in large nonstick skillet over high heat. Season shrimp with salt and black pepper. Add to skillet; cook 3 minutes or until lightly browned on both sides and opaque in center. Remove to plate.
2. Combine tomatoes, onion, cucumber, half of roasted peppers and garlic in food processor; process until blended. Add tomato juice and vinegar; process until smooth.
3. Stir in remaining roasted peppers. Divide soup between glasses or bowls; top with shrimp. Garnish as desired.

New England Clam Chowder

Makes 4 servings

- 2 tablespoons butter, divided
- 4 ounces smoked turkey sausage, finely chopped
- 1½ cups chopped onions
- 2¾ cups milk
- 1 medium red potato, diced
- 1 can (6½ ounces) minced clams, drained, liquid reserved
- 2 bay leaves
- ½ teaspoon dried thyme
- ¼ teaspoon salt
- ¼ teaspoon black pepper
- Saltine crackers

1. Melt 1 tablespoon butter in large saucepan over medium-high heat. Add sausage; cook and stir 2 minutes or until browned. Remove to plate.
2. Add onions to saucepan; cook and stir 2 minutes. Stir in milk, potato, reserved clam liquid, bay leaves, thyme and salt. Reduce heat to medium-low; cover and simmer 15 minutes or until potato is tender.
3. Remove and discard bay leaves. Stir in sausage, clams, remaining 1 tablespoon butter and pepper; cook until heated through, stirring frequently. Crumble crackers over soup.

Slow Cooker

Vegetable and Red Lentil Soup

Makes 4 servings

1 can (about 14 ounces) vegetable broth

1 can (about 14 ounces) diced tomatoes

2 medium zucchini or yellow summer squash (or 1 of each), chopped

1 red or yellow bell pepper, chopped

½ cup thinly sliced carrots

½ cup dried red lentils, rinsed and sorted*

½ teaspoon salt

½ teaspoon sugar

¼ teaspoon black pepper

2 tablespoons chopped fresh basil (optional)

½ cup croutons (optional)

**If red lentils are not available, substitute dried brown lentils.*

1. Combine broth, tomatoes, zucchini, bell pepper, carrots, lentils, salt, sugar and black pepper in slow cooker; mix well.
2. Cover and cook on LOW 8 hours or on HIGH 4 hours. Top with basil and croutons, if desired.

Potato and Leek Soup

Makes 6 to 8 servings

- 4 cups chicken broth
- 3 potatoes, peeled and diced
- 1½ cups chopped cabbage
- 1 leek, diced
- 1 onion, chopped
- 2 carrots, diced
- 1 teaspoon salt
- ½ teaspoon caraway seeds
- ½ teaspoon black pepper
- 1 bay leaf
- ½ cup sour cream
- 12 ounces bacon, crisp-cooked and crumbled
- ¼ cup chopped fresh parsley

1. Combine broth, potatoes, cabbage, leek, onion, carrots, salt, caraway seeds, pepper and bay leaf in slow cooker; mix well.
2. Cover and cook on LOW 8 to 10 hours or on HIGH 4 to 5 hours.
3. Remove and discard bay leaf. Whisk ½ cup hot liquid from slow cooker into sour cream in small bowl until blended. Add sour cream mixture and bacon to slow cooker; mix well. Sprinkle with parsley.

Grandma's Minestrone

Makes 4 servings

- 1 pound ground beef
- 1 can (about 15 ounces) red kidney beans, rinsed and drained
- 1 package (16 ounces) frozen mixed vegetables
- 2 cans (8 ounces each) tomato sauce
- 1 can (about 14 ounces) diced tomatoes
- ¼ head shredded green cabbage (about 2 cups)
- 1 cup chopped onion
- 1 cup chopped celery
- ½ cup chopped fresh Italian parsley
- 1 tablespoon dried basil
- 1 tablespoon Italian seasoning
- 1 teaspoon salt
- 1 teaspoon black pepper
- 1 cup cooked macaroni

1. Cook beef in large skillet over medium-high heat 6 to 8 minutes or until browned, stirring to break up meat. Drain fat. Transfer beef to slow cooker; stir in beans.
2. Cover and cook on HIGH 2 hours. Stir in mixed vegetables, tomato sauce, tomatoes, cabbage, onion, celery, parsley, basil, Italian seasoning, salt and pepper. Cover and cook on LOW 6 to 8 hours.
3. Stir in macaroni. Cover and cook on HIGH 30 minutes.

Cuban Black Bean Soup

Makes 4 servings

- 2 cans (about 15 ounces each) black beans, undrained
- 1 can (about 14 ounces) vegetable broth
- 1½ cups chopped onions
- 1½ teaspoons chili powder
- ¾ teaspoon ground cumin
- ½ teaspoon salt
- ¼ teaspoon garlic powder
- ⅛ to ¼ teaspoon red pepper flakes
- ½ cup sour cream
- 2 tablespoons extra virgin olive oil
- 2 tablespoons chopped fresh cilantro
- 1 lime, cut into wedges

1. Combine beans, broth, onions, chili powder, cumin, salt, garlic powder and red pepper flakes in slow cooker; mix well.
2. Cover and cook on LOW 7 hours or on HIGH 3½ hours or until onions are very soft.
3. To thicken soup, transfer half of soup to food processor or blender; process until smooth. Return to slow cooker; mix well. Turn off heat; let stand 15 to 20 minutes before serving.
4. Top with sour cream, oil and cilantro; serve with lime wedges.

Sweet Potato and Butternut Squash Soup

Makes 4 to 6 servings

- 1 pound sweet potatoes, cut into 1-inch cubes (about 3 cups total)
- 1 pound butternut squash, cut into 1-inch cubes (about 3½ cups total)
- ½ cup chopped onion
- 1 can (about 14 ounces) chicken broth, divided
- ½ cup (1 stick) butter, cubed
- 1 can (13½ ounces) coconut milk
- ½ teaspoon ground cumin
- ½ teaspoon ground red pepper
- 1½ teaspoons salt
- Sliced green onions (optional)

1. Combine sweet potatoes, squash, onion, half of broth and butter in slow cooker; mix well.
2. Cover and cook on HIGH 4 hours or until vegetables are tender.
3. Blend sweet potato mixture in batches in blender or food processor until smooth. (Or use hand-held immersion blender.) Return to slow cooker. Stir in remaining broth, coconut milk, cumin, red pepper and salt; mix well.
4. Cover and cook on HIGH 15 minutes or until heated through. Sprinkle with green onions, if desired.

Beef Fajita Soup

Makes 8 servings

- 1 pound cubed beef stew meat
- 1 can (about 15 ounces) pinto beans, rinsed and drained
- 1 can (about 15 ounces) black beans, rinsed and drained
- 1 can (about 14 ounces) diced tomatoes with roasted garlic
- 1 can (about 14 ounces) beef broth
- 1½ cups water
- 1 green bell pepper, thinly sliced
- 1 red bell pepper, thinly sliced
- 1 onion, thinly sliced
- 2 teaspoons ground cumin
- 1 teaspoon seasoned salt
- 1 teaspoon black pepper
- Optional toppings: sour cream, shredded Monterey Jack or Cheddar cheese, chopped olives

1. Combine beef, beans, tomatoes, broth, water, bell peppers, onion, cumin, seasoned salt and black pepper in slow cooker; mix well.
2. Cover and cook on LOW 8 hours. Serve with desired toppings.

Creamy Cauliflower Bisque

Makes 8 servings

- **1 pound frozen cauliflower florets, thawed**
- **1 pound russet potatoes, peeled and cut into 1-inch cubes**
- **2 cans (about 14 ounces each) chicken broth**
- **1 cup chopped yellow onion**
- **½ teaspoon dried thyme**
- **¼ teaspoon garlic powder**
- **⅛ teaspoon ground red pepper**
- **1 cup evaporated milk**
- **2 tablespoons butter**
- **1 teaspoon salt**
- **¼ teaspoon black pepper**
- **1 cup (4 ounces) shredded sharp Cheddar cheese**
- **¼ cup sliced green onions**
- **¼ cup finely chopped fresh parsley**

1 Layer cauliflower, potatoes, broth, onion, thyme, garlic powder and red pepper in slow cooker. (Do not stir.)

2 Cover and cook on LOW 8 hours or on HIGH 4 hours.

3 Working in batches, blend soup in blender or food processor until smooth. (Or use hand-held immersion blender.) Return soup to slow cooker.

4 Stir in evaporated milk, butter, salt and black pepper. Cook, uncovered, on HIGH 30 minutes or until heated through. Top with cheese, green onions and parsley.

French Lentil Rice Soup

Makes 4 servings

- **6 cups vegetable broth**
- **1 cup dried lentils, rinsed and sorted**
- **1 onion, finely chopped**
- **2 stalks celery, finely diced**
- **2 carrots, finely diced**
- **3 tablespoons uncooked rice**
- **2 teaspoons minced garlic**
- **1 teaspoon herbes de Provence**
- **½ teaspoon salt**
- **⅛ teaspoon black pepper**
- **4 tablespoons whipping cream or sour cream**
- **¼ cup chopped fresh parsley**

1. Combine broth, lentils, onion, celery, carrots, rice, garlic, herbes de Provence, salt and pepper in slow cooker; mix well.
2. Cover and cook on LOW 8 hours or on HIGH 4 hours.
3. Transfer about 1½ cups soup to blender or food processor; blend until almost smooth. Return to slow cooker; mix well. Top with cream and parsley.

Chicken Barley Soup

Makes 4 servings

- 1 medium onion, coarsely chopped
- 1 cup thinly sliced celery
- 1 carrot, thinly sliced
- ½ cup uncooked pearl barley
- 1 clove garlic, minced
- 1 cut-up whole chicken (about 3 pounds)
- 1 tablespoon olive oil
- 2½ cups chicken broth
- 1 can (about 14 ounces) diced tomatoes
- ¾ teaspoon salt
- ½ teaspoon dried basil
- ¼ teaspoon black pepper

1. Combine onion, celery, carrot, barley and garlic in slow cooker.
2. Remove and discard skin from chicken. Trim backbone from breasts. Reserve wings for another use. Heat oil in large skillet over medium-high heat; brown chicken on all sides. Place in slow cooker; top with broth, tomatoes, salt, basil and pepper.
3. Cover and cook on LOW 7 to 8 hours or on HIGH 4 hours or until chicken and barley are tender.
4. Remove chicken to cutting board; let stand until cool enough to handle. Remove meat from bones; cut into bite-size pieces. Stir chicken into soup.

Hearty White Bean Minestrone

Makes 6 to 8 servings

- 5 cups vegetable broth
- 2 cans (about 15 ounces each) cannellini beans, rinsed and drained
- 2 medium russet potatoes (about 6 ounces each), peeled and cut into ½-inch pieces
- 1 can (about 14 ounces) diced tomatoes
- 3 medium stalks celery, chopped
- 3 medium carrots, chopped
- 1 medium onion, chopped
- 2 cloves garlic, minced
- 1 teaspoon salt
- 6 cups chopped fresh kale
- 6 tablespoons shredded Parmesan cheese

1. Combine broth, beans, potatoes, tomatoes, celery, carrots, onion, garlic and salt in slow cooker; mix well.
2. Cover and cook on LOW 7 hours.
3. Stir in kale. Turn slow cooker to HIGH. Cover and cook 1 to 2 hours or until vegetables are tender. Top with cheese.

Metric Conversion Chart

VOLUME MEASUREMENTS (dry)

1/8 teaspoon = 0.5 mL
1/4 teaspoon = 1 mL
1/2 teaspoon = 2 mL
3/4 teaspoon = 4 mL
1 teaspoon = 5 mL
1 tablespoon = 15 mL
2 tablespoons = 30 mL
1/4 cup = 60 mL
1/3 cup = 75 mL
1/2 cup = 125 mL
2/3 cup = 150 mL
3/4 cup = 175 mL
1 cup = 250 mL
2 cups = 1 pint = 500 mL
3 cups = 750 mL
4 cups = 1 quart = 1 L

VOLUME MEASUREMENTS (fluid)

1 fluid ounce (2 tablespoons) = 30 mL
4 fluid ounces (1/2 cup) = 125 mL
8 fluid ounces (1 cup) = 250 mL
12 fluid ounces (1 1/2 cups) = 375 mL
16 fluid ounces (2 cups) = 500 mL

WEIGHTS (mass)

1/2 ounce = 15 g
1 ounce = 30 g
3 ounces = 90 g
4 ounces = 120 g
8 ounces = 225 g
10 ounces = 285 g
12 ounces = 360 g
16 ounces = 1 pound = 450 g

DIMENSIONS

1/16 inch = 2 mm
1/8 inch = 3 mm
1/4 inch = 6 mm
1/2 inch = 1.5 cm
3/4 inch = 2 cm
1 inch = 2.5 cm

OVEN TEMPERATURES

250°F = 120°C
275°F = 140°C
300°F = 150°C
325°F = 160°C
350°F = 180°C
375°F = 190°C
400°F = 200°C
425°F = 220°C
450°F = 230°C

BAKING PAN SIZES

Utensil	Size in Inches/Quarts	Metric Volume	Size in Centimeters
Baking or Cake Pan (square or rectangular)	8×8×2	2 L	20×20×5
	9×9×2	2.5 L	23×23×5
	12×8×2	3 L	30×20×5
	13×9×2	3.5 L	33×23×5
Loaf Pan	8×4×3	1.5 L	20×10×7
	9×5×3	2 L	23×13×7
Round Layer Cake Pan	8×1½	1.2 L	20×4
	9×1½	1.5 L	23×4
Pie Plate	8×1¼	750 mL	20×3
	9×1¼	1 L	23×3
Baking Dish or Casserole	1 quart	1 L	—
	1½ quart	1.5 L	—
	2 quart	2 L	—